BRAND BOOK

Trip to the National Parks of Japan

Planning
Japan International Broadcasting

Editing
NHK Publishing

Cooperation
Ministry of the Environment Government of Japan

Trip to the National Parks of Japan

Table of contents

Special topic
part **2**

National parks
Stories to
Experience

44

Science Column

Afterword

The world-renowned beauty of Japanese national parks

By Shiro Wakui
Distinguished Professor,
Tokyo City University

Foreword

J apan's nature is unforgiving. It is not an exaggeration to say there are threats of natural disaster around every corner. It is also ever-changing like a kaleidoscope. We owe these characteristics entirely to the mountain range that runs down the Japanese archipelago like a spine, and furthermore, to the volcanic terrain and labyrinth of currents that surround the islands.

Among the nature on these islands—which, with its miniature garden-like quality, is one of the most beautiful in the world—those areas with especially brilliant landscapes and ecosystems are recognized through the Natural Parks Act as being particularly deserving of national protection and are designated as national parks.

Although I do realize this is a gross overgeneralization, national parks in other countries like the US are entirely based on public land and tend to be artificially delineated areas that can be summarized on a single post card. Japan's national parks, on the other hand, are community-based parks that also encompass private land.

Thus, they give us a view into the unique lifestyles that have developed out of an attempt to live alongside the harshness of nature. From this, we can get a glimpse of how much respect people have for this harsh nature and how much care and attention has historically gone into following a lifestyle or method of land use that does not incur its wrath. From how settlements and crop fields are set up to local foods and customs, these parks are full of intricate appeal that can hardly be summarized on a single post card. Visitors can start by reveling in the beauty of the nature, then open a window onto people's coexistence with such nature through the local food, and finally get in touch with the unceasing story of how people have made such a coexistence possible.

For the Japanese people, nature is at times a god. That is why it is important that humans do not do anything to harm nature for their own ends. This philosophy is not only expressed intangibly as a reverence for the natural landscapes where the gods reside, but also manifests itself in people's spatial relationship with nature, such as the way they use land.

The parts of nature mainly designated for human use—sato (living area), nora (arable land for plants that require plowing), nobe (arable land for plants that do not require plowing), and satoyama (border area between the foothills and arable flat land)—are diligently maintained, creating optimal conditions for the nature within that land to regenerate after some time. The area beyond satoyama, on the other hand, is spatially delineated into sotoyama (interior mountains), okuyama (exterior mountains), and take (mountain peak), and is carefully conserved by avoiding frivolous use while staying prepared for natural disasters. This same principle is also applied to the sea, which is divided into hama (beach), iso (shore), uchi-umi (inland sea), and soto-umi (open sea).

In a sense, Japan's national parks can be considered a physical representation of the respect that the Japanese have for nature, the respect shared not only by the people who live within the designated area of national parks, but also the wider surrounding region. The traditional philosophy of living in harmony with nature both forms the background of and is reflected in these beautiful landscapes. That is the defining characteristic of Japanese national parks.

Experts of the field and others are currently pushing forward with the "Project to Fully Enjoy National Parks,"* an effort to figure out how to answer the inbound demand to gain an appreciation for the unique appeal of such national parks. One point I have continuously made through this process is, if our aim is to promote the unique appeal of Japanese national parks such as those I have discussed so far, we must not only focus on increasing the number of visitors, but also on the invigorating economic benefits to local communities by considering promotional measures that increase overall volume (i.e. number of visitors to the region amount of money spent per visitor). In terms of the way these parks are to be enjoyed, especially as it relates to the facilities for enjoying landscapes and views, I argued that we should reject an additive mentality, and instead adopt a "less-is-more" philosophy by doing away with unnecessary facilities that give visitors a man-made impression.

Until now, those in charge of maintaining national parks have always stood on the side of nature and made steady efforts to protect and preserve it. The results of this effort have evoked a desire on the part of people both inside and outside the country to experience the romantic landscapes of this country as well as the physical representations of a philosophy that seeks to live side-by-side with nature. In this sense, national parks are both tangible natural landscapes and an intangible cultural heritage that reflects the ingenuity of the people who have lived amid the harshness of nature.

Those involved in maintaining national parks, along with those who live within the designated areas of the park or the wider regions that receive economic benefits from them must keep in mind that what is needed of them now is to take on this new challenge of how to provide a safe, pleasant, and educational experience for the people who hope to experience these parks.

* See page 45.

5

Relish exquisite nature with a trip through national parks

The true pleasure of travelling in Japan is enjoying the diversity of its ever-changing nature. Take just a short train ride, and you will find yourself looking out at a completely different landscape. Having formed at the meeting point of four tectonic plates, the Japanese archipelago has wide variations in its geology due to its origin, with different types of soil and landforms as well as vegetation and fauna in its mountains and forests, making for a diverse natural landscape. To kick off the first chapter of our journey to relish Japan's nature, we introduce our readers to three unique national parks.

Fall foliage at Tsutanuma Pond
(Towada-Hachimantai National Park)

Daisen-Oki N

Mountains and islands linked with the gods and myths

Stretching over the Tottori,
Shimane, and Okayama prefectures,
Daisen-Oki National Park
features diverse landscapes
consisting of four regions—
the mountainous area
from Mt. Daisen to Mt. Hiruzen,
Mt. Kenashi, and Mt. Senjo,
as well as the Mt. Mitoku area;
the coastal areas of the Shimane Peninsula;
the Mt. Sanbe area; and the Oki Islands.
The tallest peak in the Chugoku region,
Mt. Daisen has long been
an object of faith whose past can be seen
in a pilgrimage trail (Daisen-michi)
that remains to this day.
With the park also encompassing
the Oki Islands,
a Global Geopark with many shrines,
and the Shimane Peninsula,
where Japanese myths take place,
Daisen-Oki National Park is an area
with a deep connection to the gods.

Daisen-Oki National Park

(24)

The number above corresponds to the maps on pages 88-93.

Mt. Daisen in Tottori Prefecture is a mountain of many faces. From Kagikake Pass, which stands at 800 m above sea level on the Daisen Loop Road, you can get a view of the southern wall of the mountain. With beech forests stretching out from its foothills, the majestic figure of the rugged, masculine Mt. Daisen is striking.

Oki Islands
Saigo Port
Beppu Port
Oki Islands Global Geopark Airport

N
0   20km

Sea of Japan

Yonago Kitaro Airport
Shichirui Port
Sakai Fishing Port

Nakaumi(Inland-Sea)
Izumo Enmusubi Airport
Lake Shinji
Mihonozeki
Masumizu Highland

Izumo Grand Shrine
Daisen-ji Temple

Hinomisaki
Nageire-do Hall

JR San-in Main line
Mt. Senjo
Mt. Mitoku

San-in Expressway
Mt. Daisen
Tottori Prefecture

Kagikake-toge pass
Hiruzen Highland

Shimane Prefecture Mt. Kenashi
Nichinan Town
Okayama Prefecture

Mt. Sanbe

Mt. Daisen

Highest peak volcano alive with the spirit of worship

A peaceful view of Mt. Daisen from the Masumizu Highlands.

Around November, pincushion flowers bloom in the Masumizu Highlands.

Right The Amida Triad statue (an Important Cultural Property) is enshrined in Amidado Hall, the oldest structure in Daisenji Temple.
Below Koyu Odate of Daisenji Temple.

Mt. Daisen, the highest peak in the Chugoku region (1,729 m above sea level), is also known as Hoki Fuji. The mountain is a symbol of the Hoki Province (Tottori Prefecture) whose majestic figure can be viewed from four sides. Interestingly, each of these views gives the beholder a different impression.

Originally formed by volcanic activity, Mt. Daisen is a volcano covered with crumbly and craggy rocks full of crevices. Even now, sand and gravel continue to collapse from the mountain. Such collapses are what formed the sharp ridgelines of the northern and southern walls.

The Natsuyama Trail offers beginner-friendly hikes, with well-maintained paths that are easy to walk on, and a route that only takes around three hours each way. Along the trail, hikers can see one of the most extensive beech forest in western Japan, Special Natural Monument-designated Daisen Japanese Yew trees, communities of alpine plants, and a wide variety of wild birds, while the summit offers magnificent views of the deep blue Sea of Japan, the Shimane Peninsula, and the Oki Islands. In 1985, the Association for the Preservation of the

Renamed "Ogamiyama Shrine Okunomiya" during the Meiji period (1868-1912), the main temple of Daisenji Temple enshrines a young Okuninushi-no-mikoto, a Shinto god. According to Head Priest Shiro Takahashi, "Every July, we conduct the Mohitori Shinji ritual where an offering of holy water and herbs collected from Mt. Daisen is placed in Okunomiya." The ritual helps heal people through the bounties of nature.

Mt. Daisen Summit was established to combat the loss of vegetation at the summit due to the ground being trodden by hikers. The One-Tree One-Stone Movement, where hikers carry stones and saplings up the trail, proved to be a success, and vegetation around the summit eventually grew back. The movement still continues to this day.

In addition, Mt. Daisen is a sacred mountain that has long been the object of mountain worship and became widely known in the 11th century as a place where mountain priests practiced asceticism. Daisenji Temple is said to have been built on the mountainside of Mt. Daisen in A.D. 718 during the Nara period. While originally a place of worship for the esoteric Tendai Mikkyo Buddhism sect whose faith was based around the worship of Amida, Jizo worship became more common since the mid-Heian period (794–1185).

Daisenji Temple reached the peak of its activity during the Edo period (1603–1868) when it had as many as 42 temples and shrines. During this time, an increasing number of people started bringing cattle and horses along the trail of pilgrimage to carry food and tributes. Since the Jizo of Mt. Daisen was the guardian of cattle and horses, a cattle and horse market was established at Daisen Bakuroza in around 1726, where at its peak, as many as 10,000 cattle and horses were traded annually.

The trail that people walked along with their cattle and horses was called Daisen-michi, which was also a trail of worship. Jizo statues can be found every 1-cho (approximately 109 m) along all the routes and continue to be an inspiration to temple visitors, just as they served as encouragement for people in the past as they walked up the trail.

A milestone Jizo statue reading "5-cho to the main temple." In the past, people relied on statues such as this to find their way to Daisenji Temple.

Above The Daisen Museum of Nature and History, a facility introducing visitors to the nature and cultural history of the Daisen region.
Below Ministry of the Environment Park Ranger Nobuhiro Ito, who is well-versed in the nature of Mt. Daisen.
Below right Isao Yoshino, deputy head of the "Association for Preservation of the Mt. Daisen Summit."

Daisen Okowa (a glutinous rice dish) is a traditional food of the Daisen region frequently eaten at the horse and cattle market and by visitors of Daisenji Temple.

Japanese giant salamanders, which are known as living fossils and designated as Special Natural Monuments, can be found in the foothills of Mt. Daisen. At Nichinan Town, Tottori, there are tours to go see these creatures in the wild. Tour participants wade into rivers led by tour guide Richard and researcher Jun Okada. We encountered one that was over 70 cm long.

Izumo Oyashiro Shrine

Shrine for good relationships where gods from around the country gather

The Shimane Peninsula region is home to countless old shrines enshrining various deities, the center of which is the Izumo Oyashiro Shrine.

The shrine is dedicated to Okuninushi-no-Okami, a deity also widely known as "Daikoku-sama," who is enshrined in shrines around the country. Okuninushi-no-Okami is said to have built the nation by travelling around Japan to cultivate the land and bestow crucial knowledge upon people in the areas of farming, fishing, industry, and medicine. He is known as the deity of good relationships, granting people good relationships in many areas including between a man and a woman, in one's work, or with one's house or land.

Once the nation had been built, Okuninushi-no-Okami granted it to Amaterasu Omikami (in an event called *kuni-yuzuri*), the guardian deity of the Japanese people. Izumo Oyashiro Shrine is said to have been built during this time as a grand palace for Okuninushi-no-Okami.

In the old Japanese lunar calendar, the month of October is called *kannazuki* (month without gods). This is because once a year, deities from around the country are said to leave their shrines behind and converge on Izumo Oyashiro Shrine to perform sacred rituals. In Izumo, however, where the gods gather, the same month is called *kamiarizuki* (month of the gods), and a sacred ritual called the Kamiarisai Festival is performed. The Kamiarisai Festival takes place over around a week, beginning with the *Kamimukae Shinji*

(god welcoming) ritual, which is performed on Inasa-no-hama beach approximately 1 km west of Izumo Oyashiro Shrine. Once the gods have arrived, they are led by Ryujashin (sea serpent god) to Izumo Oyashiro Shrine along with a *himorogi*, a physical representation of the gods' presence. Although invisible to us humans, host of the shrine Okuninushi-no-Okami leads the gods who have gathered from around the country in the performance of sacred rituals.

Locals are said to spend the month of *kamiarizuki* quietly, so as not to disturb the gods as they perform various sacred rituals. In this region, gods and humans solemnly continue to fulfill their roles to this day.

Kaguraden Hall, where *gokito* (formal ritual prayer) and weddings take place. The giant sacred shimenawa rope seen at the front is approximately 13.6 m long and weighs 5.2 tons.

According to Izumo Oyashiro Shrine tour guide Kiyotada Koike, "When I was a kid, my siblings and I were often told not to fight during the month of *kamiarizuki.*"

Okuninushi-no-Okami also appears in many myths.

13

Mt. Sanbe

Vast grassland and six peaks centered around a crater

A view of Mt. Sanbe from Nishinohara, one of the entry points to the mountains. To the left is Mt. Osanbe, while the peak on the right is Mt. Kosanbe. Walkways are set up on the grassland, making for an easy walk.

Mt. Sanbe is an active volcano sitting in almost the center of the Shimane Prefecture on the border between Oda City and Iinan Town in Iishi District. Six peaks— Mt. Osanbe (1,126 m), Mt. Mesanbe (957 m), Mt. Kosanbe (961 m), Mt. Magosanbe (907 m), Mt. Taihei (854 m), and Mt. Hikage (697 m)— are centered around a crater (Muronouchi) within an approximately 5-km wide caldera formed through volcanic activity. The area around Muronouchi is a Special Protection Area of the national park where the collection of plants, creatures, and rocks is restricted. Apart from Muronouchi, there is also another crater called Okunoyu where Sanbe Onsen Hot Springs draws its water from.

The Sanbesan Shizenrin forest stretching from the north face of Mt. Osanbe to Muronouchi is designated as one of Japan's Natural Monuments, and has a dense population of trees such as beeches as well as Konara

and Mizunara oaks. At the foot of the mountain, there are extensive ranches and farmland used for cattle grazing. Stockbreeding was said to have started during the Edo period (1603–1868) in an effort to promote industry by the Yoshinaga Domain (Kawai Town, Oda

Kunibiki Hill is located in the Kitanohara area of Mt. Sanbe. From here, you can enjoy a view of everything from the Sea of Japan to as far away as the Shimane Peninsula. Recorded in *Izumo-no-kuni Fudoki*, the Kunibiki Shinwa legend tells the grand story of Mt. Sanbe and Mt. Daisen acting as stakes that pulled four pieces of land ranging from the west to east of the Shimane Peninsula in from the ocean.

Above Mayumi Yoshida serves her original Sanbe Burger, which is 100% made from beef and pork produced in Shimane. Although not originally from the area, Yoshida relocated to Shimane around ten years ago and opened a restaurant.
Below The Sanbe Burger restaurant has trees cut down and sells them as firewood to help maintain the grassland in the Nishinohara area. Part of the proceeds from selling firewood and hamburgers is donated to help the effort to preserve Mt. Sanbe's landscape.

Shown here is Tsurunoyu, one of two public baths at Sanbe Onsen Hot Springs. According to hot spring specialist Jun Nagao, "The hot springs at Sanbe Onsen have a high salt content, so they have great heat-retention and moisturizing properties. I would highly recommend a visit."

Satoshi Nakagawa grows wasabi near Kitanohara, a grassland area near Mt. Sanbe. After going around a giant fallen tree and down into a shady valley, we followed the road for a while before coming upon Nakagawa's lush green wasabi fields. Eighteen years ago, Nakagawa purchased and restored three wasabi fields that had been buried under the ground due to flooding. It took three years for the wasabi plants he had planted to start growing. "There is a layer of clay in this area, so the soil does not absorb water but instead wells up to the surface. The water is very clear, so it is ideal for growing high-quality wasabi." So says Nakagawa, who ships his wasabi to regular customers around the country.

City in the present day), who cleared the land of trees and turned it into grassland. Around 1963, when the area was first designated as a national park, grassland was not limited to the foothills but extended to near the peaks of Mt. Kosanbe and Mt. Magosanbe. Most houses at the time had thatched roofs, so the *susuki* (Japanese silver grass) harvested from the grassland was also used to build roofs. Mt. Sanbe's grassland is maintained thanks to the cattle that eat the grass, as well as regular maintenance efforts such as prescribed burning and mowing.

The Mt. Sanbe area is also a major producer of soba (buckwheat) and wasabi, thanks to its large temperature differences and plentiful water, and was a nationally famous producer of such products during the Meiji (1868–1912) to Taisho (1912–1926) periods. Nowadays, you can still see buckwheat fields here and there in the foothills, as well as wasabi producers who take advantage of the cold spring water to produce high-quality wasabi.

In addition, there are many trails leading up to each of the peaks that are accessible from a road that loops around the foothills, so hikers can choose from a variety of routes depending on their stamina and the season. The summit offers a 360-degree view of the area, giving one a visceral feel for the Kunibiki Shinwa legend in which Mt. Sanbe is said to have acted as a stake that "pulled together" the surrounding land.

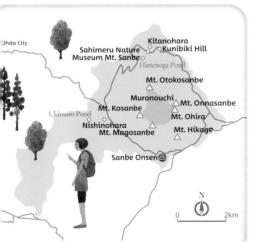

Ohda City

Sahimeru Nature Museum Mt. Sanbe

Kitanohara
Kunibiki Hill
Himenoga Pond

Mt. Otokosanbe

Muronouchi
Mt. Kosanbe
Mt. Onnasanbe
Nishinohara
Mt. Ohira
Ukinuno Pond
Mt. Magosanbe
Mt. Hikage

Sanbe Onsen

N

0   2km

Oki Islands

Dynamic coastlines and
a rich local lifestyle

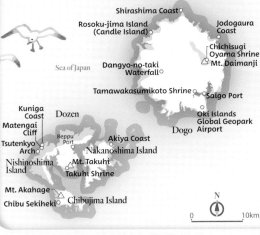

Kuniga Coast on Nishinoshima Island offers one of the most splendid views in the Oki Islands. In addition to the pictured Matengai Cliff, various interesting landforms caused by coastal erosion can be seen here, including Tsutenkyo Arch and Kannoniwa Rock.

Shirashima Coast
Rosoku-jima Island (Candle Island)
Jodogaura Coast
Chichisugi
Oyama Shrine
Mt. Daimanji
Sea of Japan
Dangyo-no-taki Waterfall
Tamawakasumikoto Shrine
Saigo Port
Oki Islands Global Geopark Airport
Kuniga Coast
Dozen
Matengai Cliff
Dogo
Beppu Port
Tsutenkyo Arch
Akiya Coast
Nakanoshima Island
Nishinoshima Island
Mt. Takuhi
Takuhi Shrine
Mt. Akahage
Chibu Sekiheki
Chibujima Island

N
0   10km

Forty to eighty kilometers north of the Shimane Peninsula in the Sea of Japan lie the Oki Islands, which consist of four inhabited islands—Dogo Island and the Dozen Islands (Nakanoshima Island, Nishinoshima Island, and Chiburijima Island)—surrounded by approximately 180 uninhabited islands of various sizes. Their beautiful coastlines and lush natural landscapes have been designated as part of a national park, and in recent years, the islands have been recognized as Oki Islands UNESCO Global Geopark for its geological history, remote island culture, and unique ecosystem.

"Thanks to Oki's unique history, there is a lot of nature and culture that remains on these islands that can only be seen on a remote island in the western part of the Sea of Japan." So says nature guide Takayuki Fukuda, who took us around the islands. Two hundred fifty million years ago, neither Oki nor Japan were islands but were instead part of the continent. As evidence of this, one can find rocks on the Oki Islands that were formed deep underground (Oki Gneiss).

Around 26 million years ago, changes in the earth's crust started causing the Japanese archipelago to gradually drift away from the continent, creating a body of water similar to a lake after the low areas of the landmass filled with water. These waters were inhabited by such creatures as alligators, whose fossils have been discovered in Oki.

The landmass then drifted farther away from the continent, turning the lake into an ocean and creating the Sea of Japan.

17

Cattle and horses graze on the hills of Nishinoshima Island. Around here, you can see the stone walls historically used for *makihata*, a technique of alternating between crop farming and stockbreeding. *Makihata* was thought up by the ancestors of the island who lived in harmony with the land.

A Darumagiku chrysanthemum (*Aster spathulifolius*), a species of continental origin, grows on the coast of Dogo Island.

The Okinoaburagiku chrysanthemum (*Dendranthema okiense*) is a native species of the Oki Islands.

High-speed ferries are a convenient option for travelling from the mainland and in between islands.

What caused Oki to surface from the bottom of the sea were volcanoes. Oki had gradually been rising until around six million years ago when explosive volcanic activity around Dogo and Dozen created the origins of the islands we see today. The depression at the center of the Dozen Islands is a caldera which also formed as the result of a volcanic eruption. Mt. Takuhi, the central cone of this caldera, is encircled by a series of islands separated by shallow waters. When it first appeared above ground, Oki was extremely rugged and covered in sedimented volcanic material, but then, as if to replace the volcanic activity, the island was subjected to the raging waters of the Sea of Japan and heavy rainstorms, causing it to erode and form the intricate coastlines and strange rock formations we see today.

Sea levels dropped during the ice age around 20,000 years ago and Oki became connected to the Shimane Peninsula by land. The subsequent warming of the earth caused sea levels to rise again, reseparating Shimane Peninsula from Oki and turning the latter into a remote archipelago around 10,000 years ago.

Fostered by this dynamic geological history, Oki has a unique ecosystem with such curiosities as cold climate plants and tropical plants growing side-by-side. This unique ecosystem extends to insects and animals as well. Consider searching for some of these "curiosities of Oki" as you go around the islands.

The oddly shaped "Candle Rock (Rosoku-jima Island)" stands off the north-west coast of Dogo Island. Whenever a sunset lines up with the tip, the island looks like a giant candle that has been lit.

The caldera at the center of the Dozen Islands as seen from Mt. Takuhi on Nishinoshima Island. Since it is an inland sea, there is almost no erosion caused by waves.

Forming a giant rock bridge that protrudes out into the sea, Tsutenkyo Arch was created by the middle rock portion eroding and getting gouged out by the sea. The pathway leading from Tsutenkyo Arch to Matengai Cliff was chosen as one of "Japan's 100 finest pathways" that everyone should visit at least once. The pathway is 2.3 km or a 60 to 90-minute walk each way.

Sekiheki (red cliff) on Chiburijima Island. The rocks turned red when volcanic eruptions caused sprays of hot lava to shoot out from the earth and the iron contained in those sprays oxidized in midair. The red color is accentuated when viewed on a rainy day.

Culture fostered by the ancient people of Oki

Humans have inhabited the volcanically formed Oki Islands since ancient times, collecting and trading obsidian, which was used to make arrowheads and blades. As the only obsidian producing area in the Chugoku region, Oki's rocks were carried to places around the Chugoku region as well as Niigata and the Shikoku region since as far back as 30,000 years ago. Through trade, the people of Oki at the time are believed to have interacted with people of many different lands.

While keeping its ancient culture alive, Oki eventually became a destination for remote exile, accepting exiles from the aristocratic and bureaucratic classes, as well as emperors such as Emperor Gotoba and Emperor Godaigo. According to one theory, Oki was chosen as it was not only far from the capital, but also a place

Takuhi Shrine sits on Mt. Takuhi, the highest peak on Dozen Island, and is said to have been established before 838 A.D. Built inside a cavern, the main shrine building enshrines the god of safe sea voyages.

"Oki is a treasure trove. A lot has survived since the ice age." So says Koji Yahata, a local knowledgeable about the nature of Oki. Yahata works with obsidian by trade, a product of this nature.

Residence of the Sasaki family, shoya (village elder) of Oki, believed to have been built in 1836. The entrance and floorplan are unique to Oki. Nowadays, you can enjoy rustic traditional foods inside the house (reservation only).

where noble exiles would be safe from starvation and danger. People must have had faith in the island, as food was plentiful, and it was a historic area that had been around since the first obsidian miners.

From the mid-Edo period (1603–1868) to around 1897, Oki flourished as a port along the Kita-mae-bune trading route. In busy years, as many as 4,500 ships docked at ports around the islands. Thanks to this, Oki became a hub of information and merchandise, giving birth to a rich culture.

Oki also developed a unique culture of its own including; the Oki Traditional Sumo tournament, which was originally performed as a ceremonial offering to the gods; the *Uma-ire Shinji* ritual, in which sacred horses carrying local deities gallop up the slopes of Tamawakasu-mikoto Shrine; and *Ushi-tsuki* (Oki Bull Sumo), which first took place as a way to console an exiled Retired Emperor Gotoba.

In addition, Oki is home to many shrines, some of which pass down a form of nature worship where spirits reside within massive trees, boulders, waterfalls, or mountains instead of the usual *shaden* (shrine building). Oki's shrines can be considered the very starting point of faith in Japan, and by visiting them, one can gain an appreciation for what people in ancient times valued in their lives.

The Chichi-sugi Japanese cedar, goshintai (spirit repository) of Iwakura Shrine on Dogo Island, one of the most iconic shrines dedicated to nature worship. With its many dangling branches, the shape of the tree is believed to be the product of ancient Japanese cedar genes that remain on the island as well as the local climate.

Tamawakasu-mikoto Shrine on Dogo Island is dedicated to Tamawakasu-no-mikoto, a deity believed to be involved in the cultivation of Oki. Within the shrine grounds, one can see the Yao-sugi Japanese cedar tree, a Natural Monument believed to be approximately 2,000 years old.

Hotels and inns in Oki serve island cuisine made from local ingredients. The Cocoro Ryokan near Saigo Port on Dogo Island is a small inn run by husband Jun Ishizuka and wife Mayumi.

Oyama Shrine (Dogo Island) is dedicated to the worship of giant trees and boulders. Vines collected from the mountain are wrapped around a sacred tree for the Fuse Mountains Festival, a ceremony to pray for the safety of people who work in the mountains.

According to tour guide Kazushi Saito, "Oki has around 100 shrines."

Many of the forests within Towada-Hachimantai National Park have deciduous broad-leaved trees such as beeches and Mizunara oaks. These trees have excellent water-retention properties that prevent floods and droughts, and provide people with tasty drinking water by purifying it of dirt.

Towada-Hachima

Blessings of beech forests and high-quality hot springs

Located in the mountainous area in the northern part of the Tohoku region, Towada-Hachimantai National Park consists of the Towada-Hakkoda and Hachimantai areas, and is a park of volcanoes, lakes, and streams. The Towada-Hakkoda area offers diverse landscapes through all four seasons with such attractions as the serene Lake Towada, the refreshing Oirase Gorge, and the Hakkoda Mountain Range, which consists of multiple volcanoes. The Hachimantai area has one of the most extensive volcanic terrain in the country and heavy snowfall. The area is dotted with lakes, marshes, and moors that formed over a long period of time, as well as hot springs with ample supplies of water.

ntai National Park

Lake Towada

Enjoy canoeing in a cauldron-shaped caldera lake

Extending over the Aomori and Akita prefectures, Lake Towada is a caldera lake formed by volcanic activity that began at the Towada volcano around 200,000 years ago. A caldera lake is formed when a volcano erupts and its crater collapses, creating a large cauldron-like depression (caldera) which fills up with water and becomes a lake. Although not apparent from the surface of the lake, Lake Towada is actually a rare double caldera that has two kinds of depressions at the bottom of the lake caused by multiple volcanic eruptions.

The calderas began to form some 55,000-15,000 years ago following a period of continuous large-scale eruptions. These eruptions caused the center part of the volcanoes to start collapsing, creating the origins of the lake we see today by forming a caldera in almost a perfect square. This was followed by the rim of the caldera collapsing, causing a massive flood that created the Oirase Gorge.

Eventually, the bottom of the collapsed caldera filled with magma, and a small volcano (Goshiki-iwa volcano) was formed at the lake bottom through intermittent eruptions. After continuous eruptions at the peak of the volcano, an eruption occurred at the side of the mountain around 7,500 years ago, forming the Ogurayama lava dome. Then, around 6,000 years ago, a giant eruption occurred at Goshiki-iwa volcano, which is believed to have formed the Nakanoumi caldera.

Thus, the double caldera lake was born, and a beech forest grew around its rim. Since there are no rivers that open onto Lake Towada, it is believed that the lake filled up from a subterranean river of rainwater and snowmelt that was retained under this beech forest on the rim of the caldera. The plentiful water of Lake Towada is carried by a man-made aqueduct in the mountains to the downstream of Oirase River where it is used for hydroelectric power generation before being used for other purposes such as farming. As a naturally-made dam, Lake Towada

The best way to enjoy a quiet moment in nature is by riding a Canadian canoe. Towadako Guidehouse Kai, which sits by the lake, conducts tours where you can learn about the history and natural ecosystems of Lake Towada while enjoying a canoe ride. Fishing is also allowed on the lake, but requires the payment of a fee.

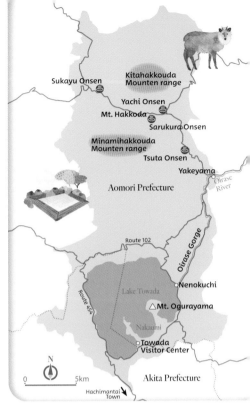

Kitahakkouda Mounten range

Sukayu Onsen

Yachi Onsen

Mt. Hakkoda

Sarukura Onsen

Minamihakkouda Mounten range

Tsuta Onsen

Yakeyama

Oirase River

Aomori Prefecture

Route 102

Oirase Gorge

Route 454

Lake Towada

Nenokuchi

△Mt. Ogurayama

Nakaumi

Towada Visitor Center

N

0   5km

Akita Prefecture

Hachimantai Town

does not only provide us with beautiful views but also contributes to people's lives.

Lake Towada sits at 400 m above sea level, has an approximately 46-km perimeter and a maximum depth of 326.8 m. It is the 12th largest lake in Japan by area and the 3rd deepest. With its mystical deep-blue surface, this serene lake is visited by many tourists all year round.

In addition to the fresh green of early summer and the fall foliage season, the lake is also very beautiful in the piercing cold of mid-winter. The lake gives one a different impression when viewed not just from a distance, but from a lower angle by actually being on the lake. One way to accomplish this is by riding a canoe, which can be enjoyed regardless of the season. This will allow you to see the many faces of Lake Towada; in the morning, when the misty lake surface glows gold; at midday, when sunlight glitters on the surface of the water; and at twilight, when countless stars start to twinkle in the sky.

A view from above makes it clear that Lake Towada is one big caldera lake.

This is a kind of freshwater salmon called himemasu which was brought over from its natural habitat in Lake Akan and Lake Chimikepp and released into Lake Towada. Some restaurants by the lake serve himemasu cuisine such as sashimi and oshizushi (pressed sushi).

25

Oirase Gorge

A nature park to walk through and stand still in

Nature guide Kawamura knows everything there is to know about Oirase Gorge. His tours include one that is solely dedicated to observing moss.

Oirase Gorge has many waterfalls. Pictured is Choshi Otaki Waterfall, the only waterfall that flows into the main current of Oirase River (the rest all flow into tributaries). The waterfall is 7 m tall and 11 m wide.

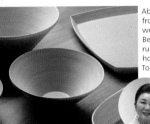

Above: Dishware made from the natural beech-wood of Aomori Prefecture. Below: Yoko Tanaka, who runs a shop that sells handicrafts from the Tohoku region.

Lake Towada, which stands on top of a mountain, has just one river flowing out of it. The river itself is called Oirase River, but the approximately 14-km scenic area—stretching from Nenokuchi, the mouth of the river, to Yakeyama, the point at which the river meets Tsutagawa River, which flows from the Hakkoda Mountain Range—is known as Oirase Gorge. In terms of elevation, the upstream area (closer to Lake Towada) is around 400 m, while the downstream area is around 200 m.

The origins of this gorge were formed around 15,000 years ago when a massive flood occurred at Lake Towada. Due to a rise in the water level at Lake Towada, the shore of the lake collapsed, scraping away a plateau of pyroclastic flow and forming the U-shaped gorge we see today.

A woodland path was first set up along the river in 1903. This was the same year himemasu fry were first released into Lake Towada.

Five years later, travel writer Omachi Keigetsu (1869-1925) visited the gorge, writing in a magazine, "One cannot say they have visited Lake Towada without seeing this gorge." This article helped the previously little-known Lake Towada and Oirase Gorge bring into the spotlight.

Nature guide Yuichi Kawamura tells us, "When walking the gorge, I recommend going upstream toward Lake Towada. By going up the gorge, you can continuously see the water flowing down ahead of you."

Oirase River maintains a constant water level regardless of the season. This is thanks not only to the water flowing in from Lake Towada but also the spring water that flows out from the beech forest atop the slopes on either side of the river. Rainwater and snowmelt are retained under the beech forest before flowing out as waterfalls of various sizes, adding color to the gorge. The accumulation of fallen leaves on the forest floor acts like a sponge and retains water like a dam. In addition, a moist wind (Yamase) blows over the mountains on the Pacific Ocean side of the Tohoku region and into the area from the mid-June rainy season to early summer, causing lots of fog and drizzle in Oirase. This moisture is trapped in the gorge, providing a healthy amount of humidity.

Around the gorge, you will see many fallen trees, but as long as they are not blocking any roads or pathways, they are left untouched. The fallen trees eventually decay, allowing various fungi to grow and microorganisms to breed, enrichening the soil. Once moss starts to grow, a tree will grow on top of it and become a home to small insects, which also attract birds and small animals. Trees that fall into the river can sometimes change its flow, and the subsequent change in the ecosystem also affects creatures like fish and aquatic insects. These are just a few examples of the dramatic moments in nature you may come across if you take your time to walk around Oirase Gorge while occasionally stopping to take a look around.

Around 300 kinds of moss grow in Oirase Gorge. A magnifying glass is a must-have item to observe tiny mushrooms and delicate growths of moss. It also comes in handy when taking pictures with a smartphone.

Hachimantai

Where traditional therapeutic hot springs used for recuperation remain

Hachimantai
Visitor Center
Lake Towada
Onuma Onsen
Tamagawa
Onsen
Fukenoyu Onsen
Obuka Onsen
Goshogake Onsen
Shin-Tamagawa
Onsen
Toshichi Onsen

Akita Prefecture

Iwate Prefecture

Matsukawa Onsen
Mt. Iwa

Amihari
Onsen

Nyuto Onsen
Village

Mt. Akita-
Komagatake

Lake
Tazawa

Kunimi Onsen

N

0   5k

Tamagawa Onsen hot spring opened in the early Edo period (1603-1868). Each minute, as much as 9,000 liters of hot water (98 degrees Celsius) gushes out from Obuki, the source of the hot spring. This hot water forms an approximately 3-m wide stream that flows into the main bath of the inn.

S tretching over the Iwate and Akita prefectures, the Hachimantai area is made up of multiple volcanoes that started erupting around one million years ago. Most notably, Mt. Hachimantai (1,613 m above sea level) has multiple craters at its summit that were created from steam explosions, which subsequently formed crater ponds such as Hachimannuma Pond, Gamanuma Pond, and Meganenuma Pond after filling up with water. The summit is a plateau with extensive marshland due to the heavy snowfall, and is a treasure trove of alpine plants.

More than anything, this area has excellent hot springs. Since the area has a high concentration of volcanoes, gas discharges and hot spring fountains as well as mud volcanoes can be seen at Goshougake-Onsen, Fukenoyu, Toshichi-Onsen, and Tamagawa Onsen hot springs. The Hachimantai area has been a popular destination for toji (hot spring therapy) since olden times, and still has traditional inns dedicated to it operating in the area. Toji is an old Japanese therapeutic method where people stay at inns for extended periods to recover both mind and body through the healing powers of hot springs. In the past, these inns were also routinely visited by elderly farmers who would come during the off-season to heal parts of their body that ached. Guests bring and cook their own food, so the inns also have communal kitchens.

In addition to these traditional inns, there are newer variations of hot spring inns that are better suited to the busy modern person. Aimed at alleviating lifestyle diseases, relieving stress, and recovering from fatigue over a two to three-day stay, these recreational hot springs allow visitors to recuperate through hot springs as they enjoy food made from local ingredients such as vegetables, meat, and fish, and take in the nature of the surrounding area while learning about its history and culture.

Above The Onuma Nature Observation Trail near Hachimantai Visitor Center. The marshland areas are fixed with wooden footpaths to protect plant life and are partly accessible by wheelchair.

Below Surrounded by a beech forest, Fukenoyu hot spring is one of the most famous hot springs in Hachimantai. Right in front of the bath, you can see the hot spring source that has been steadily flowing for over 300 years.

One of the only hot springs in the world with hydrochloric acid as its main component, Tamagawa Onsen hot spring has a pH of 1.2, or an acidity around 2 to 2.5 times higher than a lemon. The hot spring is believed to help strengthen the immune system, and has been visited by many people seeking to receive toji therapy, both in the past and present. The hot spring itself was born toward the end of the Nara period (710-794 A.D.) out of a massive explosion at Mt. Yakeyama (1,336 m), but due to its location in the mountains, people have only bathed in it since the early Edo period. In the present day, a nature observation trail is set up near the hot spring source where you can observe hot spring fumaroles and the billowing hot spring source as you take a walk. While Tamagawa Onsen hot spring is a traditional inn, sister facility Shin-Tamagawa Onsen hot spring is nearby, where visitors can stay in a resort-like setting while enjoying the same hot spring water to their heart's content.

Above There are 14 kinds of indoor baths at Shin-Tamagawa Onsen hot spring including a bath that contains 100% water from the hot spring source as well as one at 50%, a bubble bath, a low-acidity bath, and a seated bath, as well as an indoor hot stone spa.
Below Manager Shinichi Abe tells us, "Shin-Tamagawa Onsen hot spring is also open during the winter."

Above Popular as a mountain hot spring resort destination, Shin-Tamagawa Onsen hot spring has a modern, mountain lodge-style exterior.
Above right Furnished with tatami mats and twin beds, the guest rooms are cozy spaces with wood-filled interiors.
Below right Meals are buffet-style, offering foods made with health and beauty in mind. There are also special menu items, like the pictured Akita beef teppanyaki (food cooked on an iron grill).

Akan-Mashu

Akan-Mashu
National Park
③

Kushiroshitsugen
National Park
④

+Kushiroshitsugen N

National Park

Mystical nature and Ainu culture

The foundation of Akan-Mashu
National Park is made up
of caldera landforms
which were created through
multiple large volcanic eruptions.
The calderas filled with water,
forming Lake Akan, Lake Kussharo,
and Lake Mashu.
A dense forest grows around these lakes
as if to envelop them, and is inhabited
by wild animals such as Yezo deer,
brown bears, and Ezo red foxes.
The park continues to experience
volcanic activity, and as a result,
is also blessed with many hot springs.
On the shore of Lake Akan,
there is a settlement where the indigenous
Ainu people live, which allows you to get
in touch with an Ainu culture that has lived
in harmony with nature.
In addition,
Kushiroshitsugen National Park—
a wetland where water flows
in from Kushiro River,
whose headwater is Lake Kussharo—
provides a rare habitat for many plants
and animals including
the Japanese crane,
a Special Natural Monument.

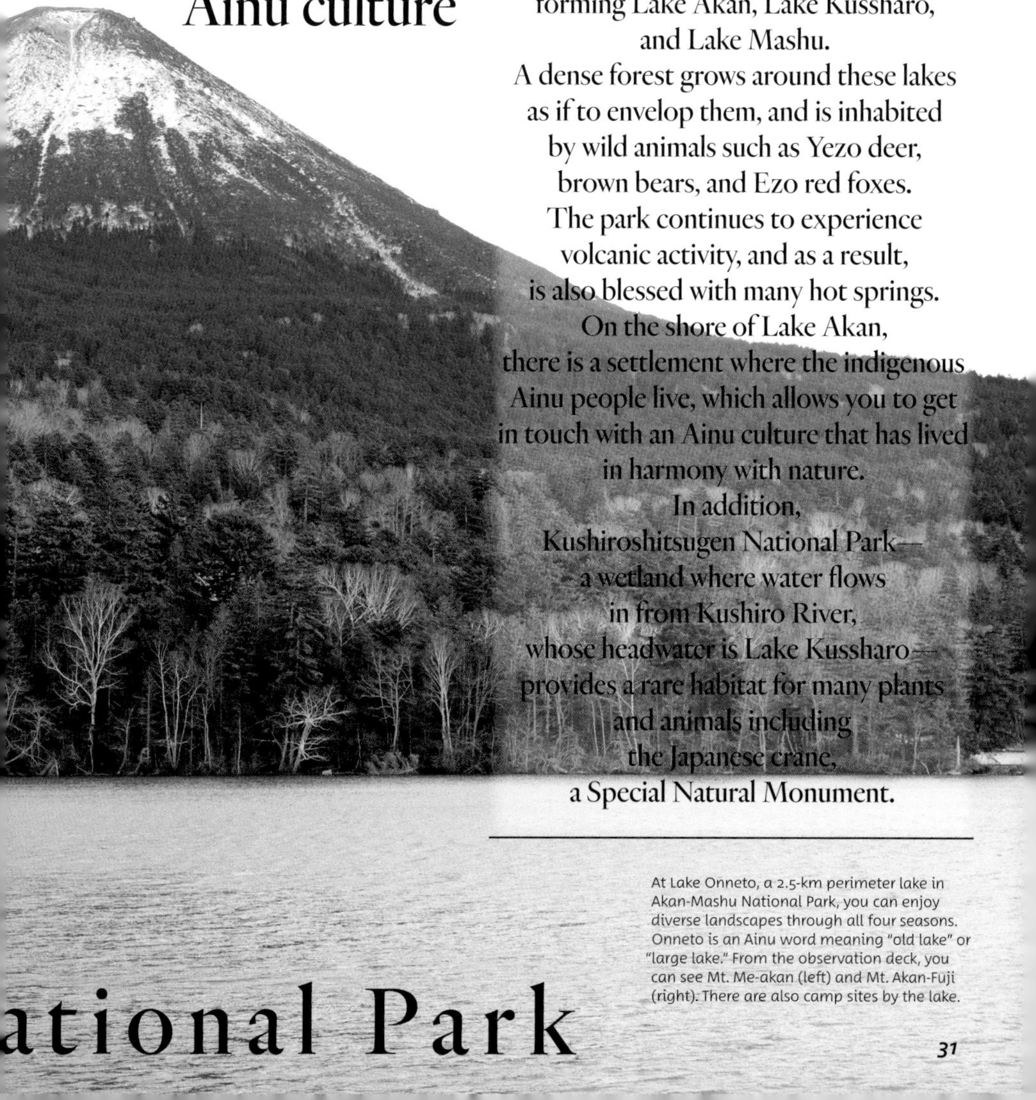

At Lake Onneto, a 2.5-km perimeter lake in
Akan-Mashu National Park, you can enjoy
diverse landscapes through all four seasons.
Onneto is an Ainu word meaning "old lake" or
"large lake." From the observation deck, you
can see Mt. Me-akan (left) and Mt. Akan-Fuji
(right). There are also camp sites by the lake.

ational Park

Lake Kussharo, Lake Mashu, and Lake Akan

Dense forests created by volcanoes and unique lakes

Above The largest caldera lake in the country, Lake Kussharo's name stems from the Ainu word *kutcharo* (throat).
Middle Standing on the shore of Lake Kussharo, the popular Kotan Onsen hot spring allows visitors to bathe at lake surface-level.
Right At Sunayu (sand bath), hot springs flow out when you dig up the sand on the lakeshore. During winter, you can also see whooper swans gather here.

Ministry of the Environment ranger Yukiko Kobayashi works to communicate the appeal of Akan-Mashu National Park.

The Kawayu Eco Museum Center at Kawayu Onsen hot spring. A café on the second floor allows visitors to look out at the Sakhalin spruce forest as they enjoy a tasty cup of coffee.

Near the Center you will find Kawayu Onsen's footbath, which can be casually enjoyed by all visitors.

Standing on the shore of Lake Kussharo, Wakkanupuri is a hot spring inn that serves just one group of guests a day. Their biggest selling-point is the Japanese cuisine they serve made with local ingredients. Owner Tomomi Shimazu tells us, "We would like our guests to think of us as a holiday home and relax." The inn has two guest rooms with modern designs—one western-style and one Japanese-style room—which look out onto Lake Kussharo. The rooms have wooden outdoor baths in addition to indoor baths.

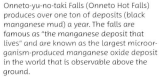

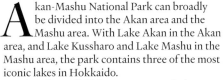

Onneto-yu-no-taki Falls (Onneto Hot Falls) produces over one ton of deposits (black manganese mud) a year. The falls are famous as "the manganese deposit that lives" and are known as the largest microorganism-produced manganese oxide deposit in the world that is observable above the ground.

Lake Akan, which is famous for its Marimo moss balls (see page 37).

The view from the Lake Mashu 1st Observation Deck. On the right end, you can see the large crater of Mt. Mashu, also known as Kamuinupuri (god's mountain). The lake is famous for its mist, a phenomenon caused by a sea fog that forms out at sea on the Pacific Ocean during the summer and covers eastern Hokkaido, which comes over the surrounding mountains and flows into Lake Mashu after forming a mass of thick mist.

Akan-Mashu National Park can broadly be divided into the Akan area and the Mashu area. With Lake Akan in the Akan area, and Lake Kussharo and Lake Mashu in the Mashu area, the park contains three of the most iconic lakes in Hokkaido.

These beautiful lakes were created when volcanic activity in the Chishima Volcanic Zone created a large depression and the caldera filled up with water. The terrain of the park, where multiple pairs of volcanoes and lakes stand in close proximity—such as Lake Mashu and Mt. Mashu, and Lake Akan and Mt. O-akan—is rarely seen throughout the country. At the Akan caldera, eruptions that occurred a few hundred-thousand to 150,000 years ago formed the Ko-akan (old Akan) lake before it was split up from an eruption at Mt. O-akan (1,370 m above sea level) around 10,000 years ago, creating the lakes we see today—Lake Akan, Lake Penketo, and Lake Panketo. These lakes are surrounded by the Mt. Me-akan (1,499 m), Mt. O-akan, Mt. Fuppushi (1,225 m), and Mt. Kikin (995 m) volcanoes.

The Kussharo caldera is said to have originated from a massive eruption that occurred around 130,000 to 100,000 years ago. Lake Kussharo, the largest caldera lake in the country, sits in the center of this caldera, surrounded by the majestic Bihoro Pass and Mt. Mokoto on the rim of the caldera, as well as Mt. Iwosan (a.k.a. Atusanupuri, see page 34) on the foothills, out of which white smoke continues to billow to this day. In mid-winter, you can observe various natural phenomena that are unique to the extreme cold climate, most notably the curious *omiwatari* (crossing of the gods) phenomenon, where ice on the frozen lake surface bulges up.

The Mashu caldera was formed around 7,000 years ago from a massive eruption and contains Lake Mashu, one of the clearest lakes in the world. On the southeast wall of the caldera, you will find Mt. Mashu (857 m) whose magnificent explosion crater is striking, and to the southeast of that, you can see Mt. Nishibetsu (800 m), a mountain famous for its treasure trove of alpine plants.

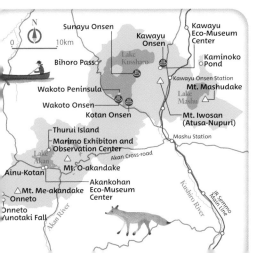

Mt. Iwosan
(Atusanupuri)

Feel the beating of the earth from an active volcano that shoots out gas

Left A trekking tour of Mt. Iwosan will give you the chance to learn about the history of the mountain. The tour lasts for around three hours.
Right Certified guide Shinobu Katase. There are tea breaks to look forward to on the mountain.

Above The thrilling fumarole shoots out gas at close to 100 degrees Celsius, so caution is required.
Below A kind of lichen called reindeer lichen, which thrives even in the acidic soil that contains high amounts of sulfur. Notice the "red lips" at the tip known as the "Monroe Lip."

Lying to the east of Lake Kussharo, Mt. Iwosan (508 m) is a mountain that continues to shoot out volcanic smoke to this day, whose Ainu language name is Atusanupuri, meaning "naked mountain" (due to its lack of any vegetation or trees). With a strikingly desolate hillside, this mountain was utilized as a sulfur mine from the early Meiji period (1868-1912) to the mid-1960s. Demand for sulfur was rising at the time, as it was used to make matches and gunpowder, and mining took place at Mt. Me-akan as well.

It was the Ainu people who first created the opportunity for sulfur mining. Hearing that the Ainu used sulfur for kindling, Kushiro merchant Sano Magouemon prospected for the mineral before setting up a full mining operation. The operation was later handed over to Yasuda Zenjiro, founder of the Yasuda *zaibatsu* (business conglomerate), who further expanded the business through such measures as constructing a railroad to improve efficiency. However, business did not prosper for long; the mining operation was shut down in 1896, and the approximately 40-km long railway was sold to the Hokkaido Prefectural Office (currently used as part of the JR Senmo Line). Various entrepreneurs attempted to set up mining operations from the late Meiji to Taisho (1912-1926) periods, but finally in 1963, the mountain was shut down and has been inoperative ever since.

Mt. Iwosan became widely known for its sulfur mining operations, and industry boomed in the previously all but uncharted eastern Hokkaido region, providing a foundation for the development of the region after experiencing an influx of many workers. Visitors can see volcanic smoke rising from the fumarole of the mountain up close by walking to it from the parking lot where the rest house is located. This view is dynamic enough, but if you have the time, we definitely recommend taking a hike up the mountain. Hiking was prohibited at Mt. Iwosan until recently, when trekking tours conditioned upon being led by a certified guide were developed, allowing people to hike up the mountain if they participate in the tour. By actually walking on the hillside as you think back to its past as a sulfur mine, you will get a feel for the important role that Mt. Iwosan has played in the history of this region. At the foothills you will find Kawayu Onsen hot spring, which is known for its highly acidic sulfur-based hot spring that can be traced back to Mt. Iwosan. The hot spring has an overflowing supply of ample water that flows into a river and sends up steam. With its sulfur content providing excellent bactericidal properties as well as heat-retention effects, this hot spring has also been a popular toji hot spring therapy destination since olden times.

Mt. Iwosan is still active to this day.

Ainu culture

Lifestyle of the Ainu people that coexist with nature (gods)

Folk Ainu handicrafts found in a folk handicraft store in Akanko Onsen Town.

At Lake Akan Ainu Theater Ikoro, you can enjoy such performances as the ancient Ainu ceremonial dance. The Ainu people have historically expressed their joy and sorrow through song and dance. These performances are always imbued with a sense of gratitude and respect toward the gods and their ancestors.

Traditional Ainu recipes have a home-cooked taste that has been handed down from generation to generation. Ohaw soup contains ingredients such as deer meat (Traditional Ainu Food Café Poronno).

Masao Nishida (left) runs a folk handicraft store in the Ainu Kotan settlement (right). His traditional dress is embroidered with *moreu* (spiral) and *aiushi* (thorn) patterns.

At Akankohan Eco-museum Center, you can learn about Marimo and Ainu culture in addition to the nature of the Akan area.

According to Marimo researcher Yoichi Oyama, "When Marimo grow large, the algae near the middle dies, creating a cavity like this" (bottom right picture). Marimo are made from a large collection of thin, three to four-cm long algae filaments. These are tossed around at the lake bottom by waves, eventually forming a ball. Marimo that have grown large are washed ashore where their spherical shape falls apart, and new Marimo are formed from those remains. The top right picture shows the process by which these pieces of Marimo grow into a sphere over an approximately seven-year cycle. On the left is a tank of large Marimo in the Marimo Exhibition and Observation Center on Churui Island.

All around Hokkaido, there are settlements of the indigenous Ainu people. The Ainu, who believe gods reside in all parts of the natural world, have historically worshipped nature, calling it *kamuy*. To distinguish themselves from the kamuy, they call themselves Ainu, which means human, and the places where they live Ainu Moshir (quiet land on which humans reside).

For the Ainu, nature encompasses not just forests, rivers, lakes, animals, and plants, but all things that have to do with human life, including fire, water, and everyday tools like mortars and pestles. It is believed that the kamuy take on the appearance of different objects and creatures before visiting the human realm to bless humans with their bounty and be useful to them. Whenever the Ainu experienced an earthquake, tsunami, or a deadly disease, it was believed to be the work of evil kamuy. The Ainu believe that kamuy and humans are meant to live by supporting one another, and have interacted with nature under the belief that humans, as a part of the natural world, have been granted the right to live there.

For example, to us, capturing animals for their meat and fur may seem like taking an animal life, but the Ainu see it as being visited by the god whose role is to deliver fur and meat to the humans. In exchange for the bounties received from the animal, the Ainu give various offerings and express gratitude by conducting a ceremony to send the gods back to their realm in the hope that they will visit the humans again. These ceremonies are called *iomante*, with the *kumaokuri* (bear sendoff) ceremony being one of the most famous.

These ceremonial prayers to the gods were not just conducted for living things but also for such instances where everyday tools broke down and became unusable. The Ainu have expressed their unwavering appreciation for all aspects of life and their gratitude to the gods through the unique Ainu ceremonial dances, traditional performing arts, and ceremonies that have been passed down to the present. You can experience various such Ainu culture by visiting the settlements where the Ainu people live (called *kotan* in the Ainu language) such as the one on the shore of Lake Akan.

The Marimo moss balls seen in Lake Akan, which are designated as Special Natural Monuments, are also highly valued by the Ainu people who live in Akan. Lake Akan is said to be the only place where you can see Marimo form a beautiful spherical shape. After World War II, when Marimo were on the brink of extinction, a movement rose up to protect them. Thus, in 1950, the 1st Marimo Festival took place, where people gave thanks to the gods for their daily lives as well as the lake and surrounding environment that help nurture Marimo. Ever since, the traditional Ainu Marimo sendoff ceremony is conducted aboard dugout canoes on Lake Akan each year in early October.

Kushiro Marsh

Untouched land inhabited by rare animals and plants

A major characteristic of Kushiroshitsugen National Park is that you can enjoy views with a different appeal from mountains and coastlines. Water from Kushiro River, a river whose headwater is Lake Kussharo, flows into the park, forming a spacious 63,886-acre marsh, which continues to be inhabited by a diverse array of wildlife thanks to large parts of the land being left untouched by humans. While the Japanese crane (see page 40) is the most iconic, Kushiro Marsh is also inhabited by cuckooflowers and Siberian salamanders, which are said to have survived from the ice age.

To start, get a view of the marsh from the Hosooka Observatory or the Kottaro Marsh Observatory which can be found within the park grounds. From there, you can see Kussharo River winding its way through the expansive marshland and the numerous lakes dotted throughout. The flora on the marsh can broadly be divided into three categories—reeds and sedges, sphagnum moss, and alder trees. A majority of the marshland—around 80 percent—is taken up by reeds and sedges, with reeds growing to around 2 m high while sedges to 60-80 cm. Since these areas are on lower ground than their surroundings, they are called low moors, and are consistently submerged underwater due to the inflow of water from the surrounding areas.

Underneath this surface is a dense, few-meter deep layer of peat, followed by a layer that contains mud, sand, pebbles, and such fossils as seashells. Peat is a kind of soil made up of plants that have only been partially decomposed due to low temperatures, which gradually becomes thicker each year as a new layer accumulates.

Above Yezo deer can be seen here and there in the marsh. *Middle* An Ezo red fox, with its prominent bushy tail. *Below* As a midway point to wintering spots, many waterfowl can be seen resting on lakes within the marsh during the fall. *Right* A view of the Kushiro Marsh from the Hosooka Observatory, which is located within the national park.

The cuckooflower has survived since the ice age. Around May, cross-shaped flowers of pale purple to white bloom.
©Masami Goto / amanaimages

The amount of peat produced in a year is just 1 mm, which means it takes as much as 3,000 years for 3 m of peat to develop. Peat retains water like a sponge and water seeps out when you step on it. It plays a crucial role in maintaining the marsh.

The Kushiro Marsh developed around 20,000 years ago during the coldest of the most recent ice ages. The temperature was around 10 degrees Celsius lower than it is now, and the sea level was around 100 m lower, so the area became connected to Siberia by land. The earth subsequently warmed, and the melted sea ice expanded the area of the sea (in an event called the Holocene glacial retreat), which covered the area around Kushiro

Ministry of the Environment ranger Atsuko Yabe tells us, "If you wish to explore the Kushiro Marsh, please stop by the Onnenai Visitor Center."

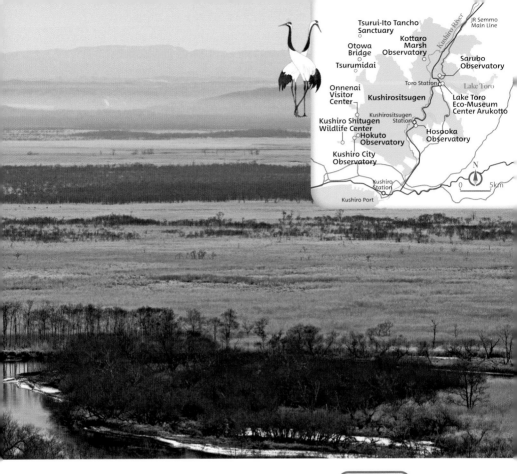

The following labels appear on the map:

Tsurui-Ito Tancho Sanctuary
Otowa Bridge
Tsurumidai
Kottaro Marsh Observatory
JR Semmo Main Line
Sarubo Observatory
Onnenai Visitor Center
Kushirositsugen
Toro Station
Lake Toro
Lake Toro Eco-Museum Center Arukotto
Kushirositsugen Station
Kushiro Shitugen Wildlife Center
Hokuto Observatory
Hosooka Observatory
Kushiro City Observatory
Kushiro Station
Kushiro Port
Kushiro River
N
0 5km

Marsh in water by around 6,000 years ago. Around 4,000 years ago, sand that had been carried to the entrance of the bay (the present-day shoreline on the west side of downtown Kushiro) started accumulating, and closed the bay off. At the same time, the earth gradually cooled, which now began to increase the amount of dry land. The bay turned into a lake, was buried under dirt and sediment, and became desalinated after experiencing an inflow of river water. Leaving a number of lakes to the east of the marsh (the present-day Lake Toro, Lake Shirarutoro, and Lake Takkobu), the Kushiro Marsh was born around 3,000 years ago.

Sedge
Rhizome
Peat
Volcanic ash (from 500 years ago)
Peat

Some sedges have stems that bulge out of the ground when the ground is frozen. The base of the stem then gets thinner by being tapered down by snowmelt. This process is repeated until a large mound 40-50 cm off the ground is formed. These are known as Yachibouzu (bald head of the marshlands). Onnenai Visitor Center has a cross section of a Yachibouzu on display, which will give you a good understanding of how they form.

On Kushiro River, which flows through the marsh, you can also enjoy canoeing. On sunny winter days, you can see glimmering hoarfrost, which make for an otherworldly view.

Sphagnum moss
Peat layer
Volcanic ash (from 500 years ago)
Peat layer
Volcanic ash (from 1000 years ago)

A layer of peat is also on display.

39

Japanese cranes

Beautiful Special Natural Monuments and "gods of the marsh"

In 1980, Kushiro Marsh became the first wetland in Japan to be registered under the Ramsar Convention. The official name of the convention is "Convention on Wetlands of International Importance Especially as Waterfowl Habitat." Japanese cranes (Tancho), whose natural habitat is marshland, were once thought to be extinct, but have since been saved by protection efforts, and can now be seen in places such as Kushiro Marsh and eastern Hokkaido.

There are said to be over 3,000 Japanese cranes on earth, around 1,800 of which make eastern Hokkaido their main habitat. The Japanese cranes that inhabit Japan are not migratory, so they can be seen all year round. Considered one of the largest birds in Japan, the cranes stand at 1.5 m, and their wingspan can be as large as over 2 m. Every year around mid-March, the breeding season begins, when male and female cranes build nests and lay eggs. The eggs are warmed for about a month before the chicks hatch (May to June). In around three

Above In addition to the Kushiro Marsh, Japanese cranes can also be seen in the surrounding areas. Cranes seemingly gather out of nowhere at the feeding ground of the Sanctuary when feeding time arrives. The cranes can often be seen intimidating each other with their warbles.

Left Similar to the crown of a chicken, the red part on the head of a Japanese crane is exposed skin. The crown expands when they are excited.

Dent corn is used to feed Japanese cranes at feeding grounds.

Tsurui-Ito Tancho Sanctuary is run by public interest incorporated foundation Wild Bird Society of Japan. Pictured is ranger Soichiro Tajima.

Otowabashi Bridge in Tsurui Village is a famous spot for taking pictures of Japanese cranes. The spot is a roosting place for these cranes, and many of them can be seen flying back here in the evening.

Once snow starts falling, Japanese cranes flock to feeding grounds in search of food. Tsurui Village has two feeding grounds called "Tsurui-Ito Tancho Sanctuary" and "Tsurumidai" where many Japanese cranes gather.

During the cold winter season, when temperatures in the marsh can get as low as negative 30 degrees Celsius, Japanese cranes spend their time in a nearby river. That is because it is warmer inside the river, which does not freeze over, and it is easier to hide from predators. When they go to sleep, the cranes curl their necks under their warm feathers and raise one of their legs while balancing on the other. In the morning, they will fly over to the feeding ground in time to be fed and return to their roosting place around sundown. Thus, the cranes stick to a regular routine.

months, the chicks will grow to around the same size as their parents and start to grow white feathers. From spring to summer, Japanese cranes feed on insects and fish in the marsh as well as plant buds and seeds, but in fall, their search for dent corn, which is used for cattle feed, brings them close to areas inhabited by humans. This is because corn is harvested on fields around Kushiro Marsh, and there are pieces of corn that have overflown and are left behind during the harvesting process.

41

Top left Author enjoying *hakomushi* (box sauna) at Goshougake Onsen in Akita Prefecture.
Bottom left Socializing with toji hot spring therapy guests at Goshougake Onsen.

The outdoor bath at Toshichi Onsen in Iwate Prefecture, which looks out at the sunrise.

Rejuvenate your mind and body with hot springs, earth's gift to humans

By Chikako Nozoe
Travel writer for hot springs and inns

In Japan, the hot spring capital of the world, a culture of *toji hot spring therapy* has been cultivated and passed down to the present. Relieving fatigue by becoming one with the power of nature in a hot spring is one of the most enjoyable aspects of traveling through national parks.

I n Japan, hot springs flow out from places all around the country. In total, there are 2,983 hot spring spots and 27,297 sources (based on Ministry of the Environment data from 2017). Part of the Pacific Rim of Fire, Japan is a volcanic country with 111 active volcanoes contained within its small territory. The common saying that there are many hot springs around volcanoes is true; if you look at a map of Japan, the distribution of volcanoes is highly similar to that of hot springs.

As such, most hot springs are the result of rainwater and snowmelt being absorbed into the hillside of a volcano and heated by magma reservoirs that are close to 1,000 degrees Celsius before shooting out along with the mineral and gas matter contained within the earth. Such volcanic hot springs

The outdoor bath at Marukoma Onsen in Hokkaido.

column

generally have higher temperatures.

On the other hand, there are also non-volcanic hot springs that flow out from areas that have no volcanoes, due to rainwater and snowmelt being warmed by subterranean heat, or trapped ancient sea water becoming heated for one reason or another.

From transparent to white, blue, green, red, orange, grey, black, and more, many are sure to marvel at the mystical, wide range of hot spring colors that nature produces.

The many faces of hot springs include ones where countless fine bubbles cling to the skin, ones that swim with *yunohana* (mineral deposits) that look like beaten egg, and ones that have a gooey layer of oil floating on the surface.

With their world-renowned natural environments that stretch from mountains and rivers to oceans, national parks contain many hot springs that combine the wild and gentle.

To give you some examples, starting from the north, there is the Marukoma Onsen Ryokan inn (Shikotsu-Toya National Park) on the shore of Lake Shikotsu in Hokkaido, which has mystical hot springs that well up at your feet. Since the natural outdoor bath is connected to Lake Shikotsu and shares water levels with its lake surface, the water can at times be so shallow that you need to lie down to bathe in it, while after heavy rain, it transforms into a standing bath that people bathe in with floats.

The Toshichi Onsen Saiunso inn (Towada-Hachimantai National Park) in Iwate Prefecture offers awe-inspiring views of the sunrise, which you can watch while bathing in an outdoor bath at an altitude of 1,400 m, the highest in the Tohoku region.

There is more to do than just sitting in a bath. At Goshougake Onsen (Towada-Hachimantai National Park) in Akita Prefecture, you can enjoy a wide variety of bathing, including *utaseyu* (hot spring waterfalls), mud baths, *hakomushi* (box saunas), and steam saunas.

The food there is cooked with hot spring steam, and guest rooms are heated from subterranean heat or *ondol* (underfloor heating). Good for such purposes as relieving nerve pain, strangers are quick to relax and become fast friends in the large ondol-heated communal room.

At Nakabusa Onsen (Chubusangaku National Park) in Nagano Prefecture, you will find a geothermal bath where you can warm your body from the subterranean heat by lying down on the ground as you would in a hot stone spa. The bath offers a completely unobstructed 360-degree view, and up above, you will see an expansive starry sky that looks as if it might just start showering down upon you.

Furthermore, Ibusuki Onsen (Kirishima-Kinkowan National Park) in Kagoshima Prefecture is famous for *sunamushi* (sand baths), where your entire body is buried under sand that has been heated from the hot spring source. The sand bath offers three times the hyperthermic effects of bathing in a bathtub, and washes away the toxins from your body along with sweat.

As has been done through toji, hot spring therapy, since ancient times, if you wish to "reset" your mental and physical fatigue to zero, I recommend the hot springs in national parks, as they allow you to receive power from mother nature. Come set out on a hot spring journey to feel the power of the earth.

Sunamushi (sand baths) at Sand Bath Hall Saraku, a day trip facility at Ibusuki Onsen in Kagoshima Prefecture.

National parks

Stories to Experience

The varied nature of Japan was not formed overnight but was instead created out of the interplay of various factors, including the formation of mountains and the climate. In some places, the way people have lived and worshipped among nature has helped form unique landscapes. The "Project to Fully Enjoy National Parks" is seeking to create an environment where such characteristics can be more fully enjoyed at eight parks designated as leading cases. Here, we will introduce our readers to five parks to go along with the three introduced in special topic #1. Together, let us unravel the stories of how these beautiful landscapes were cultivated.

The Five Peaks of Mt. Aso as viewed from the rim of the caldera (Aso-Kuju National Park)

✦ What is the Project to Fully Enjoy National Parks?

In 2016, the Japanese government drafted a Tourism Vision to help build Japan into a world-class tourist destination. Utilizing Japan's abundant tourism resources such as its nature and culture, the government is working across agencies and in cooperation with the private sector to aim for "a Japan that visitors from around the world would want to visit."
Based on this Vision, the Ministry of the Environment launched the Project to Fully Enjoy National Parks to help elevate Japanese national parks to a world-class standard. Through this project, the government hopes to deliver experiences where people can enjoy the brilliant nature and unique culture of each park and create a more welcoming environment for domestic and international tourists, thereby turning Japanese national parks into a destination where travelers from around the world, in addition to domestic travelers, will be longing to enjoy an extended stay.

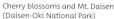
Cherry blossoms and Mt. Daisen
(Daisen-Oki National Park)

Snowshoe trekking at Lake Mashu
(Akan-Mashu National Park)

Five stories to prepare you for a trip around national parks

Japanese national parks allow you to get in touch with first-class nature such as mountains, gorges, seas, wild plants, and animals.

With a long, bow-shaped land mass that is surrounded by ocean and stretches approximately 3,000 km north to south, the Japanese archipelago is home to a wide array of natural environments, climates, and lifestyles depending on the region. Since around 80 years ago, national parks have been designated in places around the country with the aim of protecting Japan's treasured scenic areas of note and utilizing them to promote the health, recuperation, and education of Japanese citizens while securing a diverse wildlife. In 2016, the "Project to Fully Enjoy National Parks" was launched to create a high-quality welcoming environment that will not only be satisfying to the Japanese people but to a greater number of international travelers. The Project is reaching out to people around the world in the hope that they will come to admire Japan's nature and gain a more intimate appreciation for the lifestyles and culture of the Japanese people.

Before we introduce you to the five parks to go along with the three parks you saw in special topic #1, here are five stories that illustrate the characteristics and appeal of Japan's nature: diverse climatic zones, diverse wildlife, abundant water, bounties of volcanic activity, and lifestyles amid natural disasters.

Episode **01**

Distinct seasons created by diverse climatic zones

Located to the east of the Eurasian continent, Japan's territory has an area of around 380,000 km2 (excluding its maritime territory) that stretches north to south in a long bow shape and encompasses a wide array of climatic zones from subarctic to cool-temperate, warm-temperate, and subtropical. In the same winter season, some areas off the coast of Hokkaido are covered in drift ice, while in the seas around the Nansei Islands, you can see extensive coral reefs.

The majority of the country belongs to a temperate climate where the seasons are

Lake Ozenuma and the Three Larches
(Oze National Park)

distinct and nature experiences various changes through each of the seasons such as cherry blossoms in the spring and foliage in the fall. This is due to the climate being affected by changes in the seasonal winds (monsoon winds).

During the summer, Japan receives winds from the oceans to the south, making it hot and humid, while in the winter, it is visited by a dry, cold season due to the continental winds from the northwest. The summer is preceded by a rainy season and from summer to fall there are typhoons and a period of long autumn rain. In winter, a northerly wind containing moisture from the Sea of Japan causes snowfall on the Sea of Japan coast.

Thanks to this, Japan's annual rainfall is around twice the global average. This provides people with good drinking water and as such, Japan can be considered a highly water-rich country.

In addition, Japan has one of the heaviest snowfall in the world. Multiple Japanese cities are ranked within the top 10 snowiest cities of the world; Aomori City in particular, has over 7 m of annual snowfall and is number one in the world. The quality of the snow is superb, and Japan is visited by skiers and snowboarders from around the world who come in search of its high-quality powder snow.

Episode 02

Diverse wildlife with a high percentage of indigenous species

Japan has many kinds of animals and plants and is also known for having a high percentage of indigenous species.

Its relatively small land mass is inhabited by around 7,000 kinds of plants, over 1,000 kinds of animals, and 70,000 to 100,000 kinds of insects. Countries like Germany and the UK have less than half the number of wildlife

Coral reefs with highly translucent water
(Keramashoto National Park)

47

varieties and almost no indigenous species. In Japan, on the other hand, a good number of small mammals, amphibians, and reptiles, as well as around a third of the plants are believed to be indigenous.

One example of a species indigenous to Japan is the Japanese giant salamander, one of the largest amphibians in the world and a creature that has been recorded at a maximum length of 148 cm and weight of 30 kg. Japan is also inhabited by what are known as living fossils, creatures that look almost exactly like their fossils from 30 million years ago.

Bounties of abundant water

Japan's geographical position, distinct seasons brought about by seasonal winds (monsoon winds), and abundance of water help create a truly diverse landscape.

Of course, nature is not always peaceful. It can bring serious calamity to people's lives in the form of earthquakes, floods, and volcanic eruptions. At the same time, it plays an important role in people's lives by blessing them with bounties.

Rainwater in the mountains turns into spring water after being infused with nutrients from

the mountain and flows into the ocean through rivers. This sea water evaporates, forms clouds, and falls from the sky again as rain. Due to such circulations of its abundant water and its temperate climate, Japan is well-suited for agriculture and has historically grown a lot of rice. This has given birth to a rice culture and sake brewing, which form a pillar of Japanese life. Japan is truly a country cultivated and defined by its water.

Bounties of volcanic activity

Due to its position at the meeting point of tectonic plates, the Japanese archipelago experiences a lot of volcanic activity. There are two volcanic zones in the northeast and southwest that meet in the middle of Honshu (the main island of Japan) and are lined with 111 active volcanoes.

In addition to creating various landforms, volcanic eruptions have brought massive amounts of volcanic product to the surface, helping to form flatlands. Volcanic ash forms the foundation of the soil indispensable to agricultural production.

Furthermore, the cavity-filled interior of volcanoes form a subterranean river by absorbing large amounts of water, allowing spring water and groundwater to be used at the foothills. Some of the water that flows out is rich with volcanic agents, while in other cases, the subterranean heat creates a hot spring. These can be considered the bounties of volcanic eruptions.

Episode **05**

Lifestyles closely connected to nature

Why do Japanese national parks encompass commercial and residential areas?—If you have read this far, you might already have a good idea why.

It is because Japanese lifestyles, culture, and customs reflect an effort to live alongside nature, including the disasters that are caused by it.

The Japanese people have historically held a reverence for and later developed a worship toward a nature that at times brought about disaster. They have opted to live alongside it, accepting not only its bounties but also its menace by exercising their wit and ingenuity. This is symbolized in the many shrines and temples that can be seen within national parks. Worship, as well as the flow of people have helped form the unique landscapes and cultures of each region.

Some parts of nature have been protected and maintained through human intervention. These are called secondary nature, and are exemplified by *satoyama* and *satoumi*.

Satoyama are areas with paddy fields,

streams, and meadows where people live and gather surrounded by wildlife such as plants, flowers, and birds.

Satoumi are highly biodiverse coastal waters that produce plenty of aquatic resources which have historically supported culture and commerce in areas such as fishery and trade.

Satoyama and satoumi exist in the area between human habitation and nature; a rich, diverse ecosystem and natural environment is maintained through human intervention, providing us with many bounties.

By having people's lives as part of the park, we can witness the beliefs that have been passed down, the way people have lived alongside nature, and the unique nature, culture, food, and industry of each region. Such lifestyles themselves are an important resource to Japanese national parks.

Early morning canoe ride on Lake Kussharo
(Akan-Mashu National Park)

Japan's nature can be harsh and brutal but at the same time provides people with a variety of rich bounties. Amid this, people's lifestyles have developed over unfathomably long spans of time—Japanese national parks are ideal for experiencing such testaments to people living alongside nature—providing a place to get in touch with first-class nature and the essence of Japanese culture that lives within it.

Of course, it is not only important to physically maintain these landscapes but to also always keep this essence alive. If we manage to accomplish this, Japanese national parks may give each of their visitors a glimpse and feeling of how to live flexibly and gently yet resiliently in a world where values are fast-changing.

The view from Takatsukiyama Observatory on
Zamami-jima Island (Keramashoto National Park)

49

Nikko Nat

The view from the observation deck at the top of Akechidaira Ropeway where you can see both Kegon-no-taki Falls and Lake Chuzenji.

Nikko National Park

⑩

The number above corresponds to the maps on pages 88-93.

Branding Park

Relish
the beauty of
nature
and
the history

Colored by a holy mountain,
a majestic waterfall,
and a gorge known for
its beautiful fall foliage,
this area has long been
a popular summer retreat.
From shrines and temples
that are designated as
World Heritages to former foreign
embassy villas and classic hotels,
there is plenty to see
in this popular nature getaway
that is easily accessible
from Tokyo.

A nature observation trail is set up on the marshland at Senjogahara, making for a beginner-friendly walk.

A miniature garden packed with Japan's history and nature

Established in 1934, Nikko National Park is one of the most historic national parks in Japan.

A majority of the area of the park, which stretches over the three prefectures of Fukushima, Tochigi, and Gunma, is a mountainous area belonging to the Nasu Volcanic Belt with such mountains as Mt. Nikko-Shirane (2,578 m above sea level), the tallest mountain in the North Kanto region and northward; Mt. Nantai (2,486 m), which has been renowned as a mountain of worship since ancient times; and Mt. Chausu (a.k.a. Mt. Nasudake, 1,915 m), which continues to experience lots of volcanic activity. On the expansive plateaus at the foothills of these mountains is a series of lakes, waterfalls, and valleys created from volcanic activity which provide a rich tapestry of beautiful seasonal landscapes.

The park is also well-known for its shrines and temples—most notably Nikko Toshogu

There are many kinds of butterflies in this area, including the chestnut tiger.

The high-altitude Kinu-numa Swamp is a treasure trove of alpine plants. There are also hot spring inns nearby.

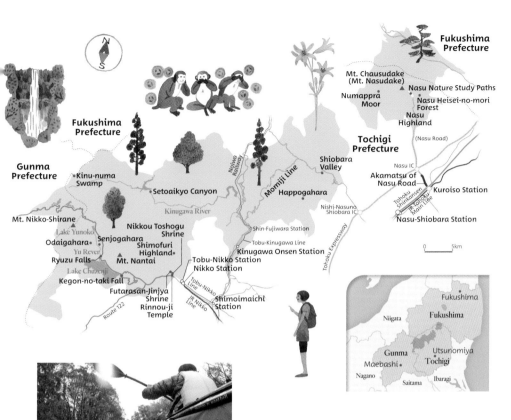

Fukushima Prefecture

Mt. Chausudake (Mt. Nasudake)

Numappra Moor

Nasu Nature Study Paths

Nasu Heisei-no-mori Forest

Nasu Highland

Tochigi Prefecture

(Nasu Road)

Shiobara Valley

Nasu IC

Akamatsu of Nasu Road

Kuroiso Station

Nishi-Nasuno Shiobara IC

Nasu-Shiobara Station

Fukushima Prefecture

Gunma Prefecture

Kinu-numa Swamp

Setoaikyo Canyon

Kinugawa River

Momiji Line

Happogahara

Mt. Nikko-Shirane

Lake Yunoko

Nikkou Toshogu Shrine

Odaigahara

Senjogahara

Shimofuri Highland

Shin-Fujiwara Station

Tobu-Kinugawa Line

Kinugawa Onsen Station

Yu River

Ryuzu Falls

Mt. Nantai

Tobu-Nikko Station

Nikko Station

Lake Chuzenji

Kegon-no-taki Fall

Futarasan-Jinjya Shrine

Rinnou-ji Temple

Route 122

Shimoimaichi Station

Niwa Railway

0   5km

Fukushima

Niigata

Fukushima

Gunma

Maebashi

Utsunomiya

Tochigi

Nagano

Saitama

Ibaragi

You can enjoy canoe tours on Lake Chuzenji and dam lakes near Kawaji Onsen and Itamuro Onsen hot springs.

Shrine—which are collectively registered as World Heritage sites, and its numerous historic structures.

Awaiting visitors with a harmonious blend of colorful natural beauty and majestic Cultural Heritages that pass on Japan's history to the present day, Nikko National Park is also easily accessible from Tokyo. As a place you can visit casually to get in touch with the Japanese essence, Nikko enjoys unwavering popularity as an established tourist destination.

Nature that transforms through each of the seasons

Lake Chuzenji, which was formed when lava flow that erupted from Mt. Nantai dammed up a river; Kegon-no-taki Falls, which falls from the mouth of this lake; and Irohazaka, a winding road with countless hairpin turns, are all notable fall foliage spots. The leaves start changing color in early October, first at the mountain peaks, then gradually down the side of the mountain as well.

Nasu-Kogen highlands have plenty of cycling routes which go through the forest.

Inside the Italian Embassy Villa Memorial Park building. Furniture from back in the day has been restored and is open to the public.

The outdoor baths at hot spring facilities offer breathtaking views.

The area offers impressive seasonal views including the fresh green of spring and fall foliage.

Nikko Toshogu, a shrine dedicated to Tokugawa Ieyasu, first shogun of the Tokugawa Shogunate. The aesthetic sensibility of 400 years ago is condensed within Yomeimon Gate, which was restored after going through large-scale reconstruction work.

Snowshoeing at Nasu Heisei-no-mori Forest. The forest offers tours accompanied by nature interpreters.

Branding Park

Nikko National Park

With Kinugawa River, Shiobara Vally, and Mt. Chausu (Mt. Nasudake) also being popular, there is no end to the plethora of spots to recommend where many people gather to enjoy fall foliage.

The winter that comes along after the fall foliage season is also highly atmospheric, with its snow-covered landscapes that extend as far as the eye can see. There are also guided tours that are quietly generating buzz where the unique winter landscape of the region such as its pristine forests and icefalls can be enjoyed through trekking and snowshoe walks.

The region is also splendid when it is colored with fresh green and flowers. There are many famous spots to enjoy flowers including the Happogahara plateau where around 200,000 Japanese azaleas grow in early summer, and Numappara Moor where you can enjoy alpine plants such as broad dwarf day lilies (Nikko Kisuge) and white hellebore (*veratrum stamineum*). Footpaths are set up around both of these spots, making for an easy hike.

During the summer, there are plenty of waterside activities to enjoy such as boat cruises down Kinugawa River, waterfall tours, and hikes along the gorge. With its colorful natural environment and dazzling panoply of beautiful seasonal landscapes, Nikko is, as it were, a miniature garden in which the natural beauty of Japan is condensed.

An area beloved through the ages

The symbol of Nikko is the Toshogu Shrine, which was built in the 17th century by third shogun of the Tokugawa dynasty Iemitsu as a dedication to his grandfather Ieyasu. The luxurious shrine was built by a team of some of the best craftsmen at the time.

Along with Nikko Futarasan-jinja Shrine, which was founded on Futarasan (Mt. Nantai) during the Nara period in the 8th century and became the central practicing site of *shugendo* (mountain asceticism) during the Kamakura period (1185–1333), Nikko Rinno-ji Temple is part of the World Heritage Site "Shrines and Temples of Nikko."

In the modern age, there was a flurry of construction on the shore of Lake Chuzenji from the Meiji period (1868–1912) to the early Showa period (1926–1989) when many foreign diplomats stationed in Japan seeking a cooler climate built holiday homes there. The area was such a popular place for foreigners in summer that it was said that "summer in Nikko was like standing in the lobby of the Ministry of Foreign Affairs." The British Embassy Villa Memorial Park and Italian Embassy Villa Memorial Park are vestiges of this age where you can stand in the exotic buildings of the former villas and think back to their past as popular, international summer retreats.

The Nasushiobara area was also popular during this time as a hot spring resort and holiday home area, and was beloved by many writers and politicians. At Nasu Heisei-no-mori, a forest previously part of the Imperial Villa that has since been opened to the public, you can enjoy rich nature that has been pristinely preserved for 90 years.

Ise-Shima N

Ise-Shima
National Park
20

A view of the ria coastline of Ago Bay from the Yokoyama Observatory in Shima City. On the ocean you can see pearl-farming rafts.

Branding Park

Home of faith and food

Known familiarly as Oise-san, Ise Jingu is surrounded by lush forests that provide a sharp contrast to the busy *monzenmachi* (shrine town). The region also has mountains and seas that provide rich bounties of food. A little way away, you can get spectacular views of the ria coastlines.

The Meoto Iwa Rocks (Married Couple Rocks) at Futamigaura. From May to July, you can watch the sun rise from between the rocks in the early morning.

Rich tapestry of *satoyama* and *satoumi* created through human activity and nature

Ise-Shima National Park extends over the Shima Peninsula, which is located in the center of Mie Prefecture.

With a spacious approximately 150,000-acre area that extends over the cities of Ise, Toba, and Shima, and Minamiise Town, the park can broadly be divided into two areas: the inland area, which encompasses Ise Jingu and the extensive forest environment that extends behind it, and the coastal area, which features intricate landforms with numerous inlets and capes known as ria coastlines.

Within the inland area there are *satoyama*, and *satoumi* spread over the coastal area. Satoyama and satoumi are natural landscapes that have been managed and maintained through human intervention, helping to create ecosystems and landscapes known as secondary nature as they interact closely with human activity such as agriculture, forestry, and fishery.

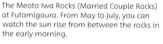

The clear water of the Isuzu River carries the nutrients of Ise's forests to the ocean.

Branding Park
Ise-Shima National Park

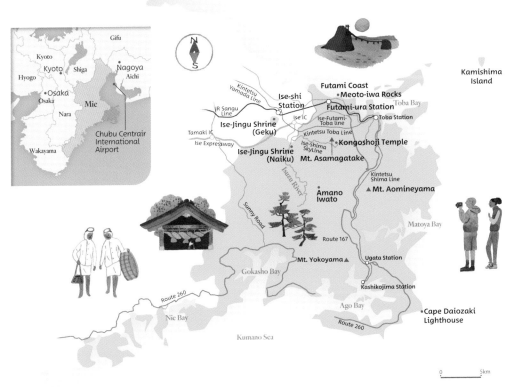

Kyoto
Gifu
Kyoto Shiga
Hyogo
Nagoya
Aichi
Osaka
Osaka Mie
Nara
Wakayama
Chubu Centrair
International
Airport

Kamishima
Island

Kintetsu
Yamada Line
Ise-shi
Station
Futami Coast
• Meoto-iwa Rocks
Futami-ura Station
Toba Bay
JR Sangu
Line
Ise IC
Ise-Futami-
Toba line
Toba Station
Ise-Jingu Shrine
(Geku)
Kintetsu Toba Line
Tamaki IC
Kongoshoji Temple
Ise Expressway
Ise-Shima
Skyline
Ise-Jingu Shrine
(Naiku) Mt. Asamagatake
Isuzu River
Kintetsu
Shima Line
Mt. Aomineyama
Amano
Iwato
Matoya Bay
Sunny Road
Route 167
Ugata Station
Mt. Yokoyama
Gokasho Bay
Kashikojima Station
Route 260
Ago Bay
Nic Bay
Cape Daiozaki
Lighthouse
Route 260
Kumano Sea

0   5km

The large *torii* gate at the entrance to the inner shrine of Ise Jingu. Once you cross Ujibashi Bridge, you are entering the realm of the gods.

What helped such coexistence and mutual prosperity of humans and nature to take root in Ise-Shima is the existence of Ise Jingu, which people of this land have worshipped at from time immemorial. Taking note of how these aspects have interacted with nature will clearly highlight the intricate appeal of this park.

© NOBUO TSUMIDA / SEBUN PHOTO / amanaimages

Beautiful grand crinum lilies (*Hamayu*) grow on Koushirahama beach.

The main palace of the outer shrine at Ise Jingu. The shrine is dedicated to Toyouke-no-Omikami.

59

In Ama fishing, Ama divers free dive to collect abalone and turbo. There are also plenty of seaweed and small fish to catch.

The Shirongo Festival in Toba City, where a pair of male and female abalone is offered to the gods to wish for a large haul and safety at sea.

Tekonezushi, which is made by topping rice with fresh seafood marinated in soy sauce, is a fisherman's dish eaten in the Shima region.

A thriving Ama fishing culture and rich bounties of the sea

The Meoto Iwa Rocks (Married Couple Rocks) at Futamigaura have been a well-known site of sunrise worship since ancient times. From May to July, the sun can be seen rising from between the two rocks. On clear days around the summer solstice (mid to late June) in particular, you can watch the sun rise from behind a faraway Mt. Fuji.

Since ancient times, people have worshipped the sun as a god. Ise Jingu is the center of such worship and consists of around 125 shrines, most notably the inner and outer shrines.

As the supplier of seafood to Ise Jingu as well as the Imperial Court in Kyoto, Shima Peninsula has historically held an important position; *waka* poems in the Manyoshu collection compiled during the 7th to 8th centuries recognize the area as "Miketsu-kuni (land that produces food offerings)." This was thanks to its rich

The sun setting
behind Kashikojima
Ohashi Bridge in
Shima City.

ocean environment and seabed landforms that nurture a great variety of marine life such as abalone, turbo, oyster, tuna, Japanese sea bream (*madai*), and seaweed.

The sea around Ise-Shima consists of a calm inland sea and the rough open waters of the Pacific Ocean. Fishing grounds in the inland sea constantly flow with the warm Kuroshio Current and have extensive "seaweed forests" along the coast of the Shima Peninsula made up of *kajime* (Ecklonia cava) and *arame* seaweed that serve as a cradle of marine life.

Ama (sea women) fishing has also thrived here since ancient times thanks to these plentiful bounties of the sea. Even now, it is said that around half of all Ama divers in Japan live in the Ise-Shima region. What has enabled such a thriving Ama fishing culture is the strict adherence to a tradition of sustainable fishing where smaller abalones are prohibited from collection and restrictions are placed on the number of days, times, and hours diving is allowed. Such reverence and appreciation for nature have also been passed down in seaweed and pearl farming.

Lifestyles of people who seek to coexist with nature

The ingenuity that the people of this region have shown as they seek to coexist with and sustain nature is also reflected in the Shikinen Sengu ritual conducted at Ise Jingu once every 20 years. The wood produced from taking down the main shrine building is reused within Ise Jingu or otherwise utilized for rebuilding and restoring shrines across the country. In addition, the Kyuikirin (precincts of the shrine) forest extending behind the shrine is systematically managed to sustainably secure the over 10,000 cypress trees that are used to rebuild the main shrine building.

Another characteristic of Ise-Shima National Park is that it contains a proportionally large area of private land compared to other national parks and is inhabited by a large population; this allows you to get a more intimate feel for the lifestyles, history, culture, and customs of the people who live in the region.

Activities you can enjoy include watching Ama fishers' skills up close as they free dive to collect shellfish and seaweed before enjoying a barbecue of the seafood they catch, sea kayaking and cycling around the ria coastlines, and a great number of ecotours where you can experience the lifestyles and culture of remote islands and fishing villages.

Ponder how humans have interacted with nature as you take in Ise Jingu and the bustle of the ancient town that surrounds it, the scenery of hills and fields, and the seaside landscapes of the Ise-Shima region. This is a place that offers such meaningful experiences.

Flowers of a Persian silk tree, which is designated as the official tree of Shima City.

Aso-Kuju N

A view of the ria coastline of
Ago Bay from the Yokoyama
Observatory in Shima City.
On the ocean you can see
pearl-culture rafts.

ational Park

Branding Park

Expansive grasslands nurtured by volcanoes and land blessed with plentiful spring water

Mt. Aso caldera seen here is among the largest in the world, but any trace of the harshness it had at the time of its eruption is gone. The area now has expansive grasslands and foothills that flow with spring water and hot springs. People here have led their lives utilizing such bounties of volcanoes. Witness the utopic coexistence of humans and nature.

Noyaki signals the arrival of spring in Aso.

Scent of the grasslands, breathing of volcanoes, and winds that frolic across the majestic landscape

Established in 1934, some of the major characteristics of Aso-Kuju National Park include Mt. Aso, which stands on a massive caldera; groups of volcanoes such as the Kuju Mountain Range that stretch to the north of the caldera; and the majestic, sloping grasslands that surround them.

At and around Mt. Aso, you can enjoy a chain of majestic views such as the Mt. Nakadake crater billowing smoke, the beautifully shaped Komezuka volcanic cone, and the floor and rim of the caldera that surround them.

There is also plenty to see around the Kuju Mountain Range such as the expansive grasslands of the Kuju Plateau and Handa Highland, as well as scientifically important wetlands such as Tadewara Moor and Bogatsuru Moor.

Stretching as wide as around 18 km east to west and 25 km north to south, the Aso caldera is among the largest in the world. Currently, there are around 50,000 people living within it, forming what is said to be the only established settlement in the world that is inside a caldera.

The soil beneath the grasslands is volcanic ash-based and low on nutrients. People have lived alongside the caldera by utilizing this land for farming and grazing.

Left unattended, the grasslands quickly turn into a forest. To prevent this from happening, *noyaki* (controlled burning) takes place all at once from late February to mid-March, creating dynamic scenes here and there in the grasslands where you can see patches of land burst into flames.

Noyaki has helped support a rare and rich ecosystem by allowing fresh grass to grow and nurturing unique insects and plants. The grasslands are also inhabited by rare butterfly species that feed off their wildflowers such as the Shijimi large blue (*Shijimiaeoides divinus*, feeds off shrubby sophora) and the scarce large blue (feeds off great burnet).

At Aso Shrine, the Hifuri Shinji (fire swinging) ritual takes place every March to pray for a bountiful harvest.

Aso's Akaushi beef cattle are raised freely as they graze on expansive grasslands.

The view from Aso's Daikanbo peak. From here, you can see both the Five Peaks of Mt. Aso to the south and the Kuju Mountain Range to the north.

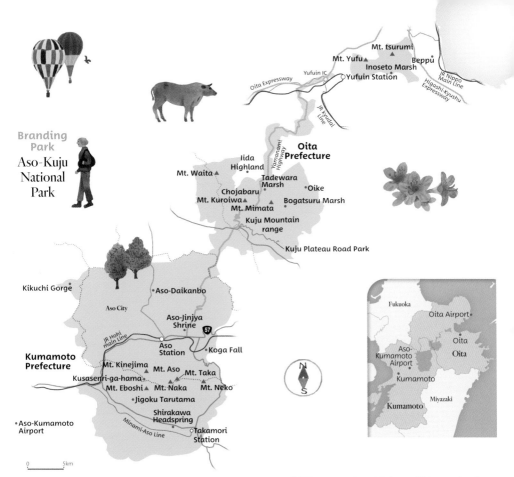

Branding Park

Aso-Kuju National Park

Mt. tsurumi

Mt. Yufu ▲   Beppu

Inoseto Marsh

Yufuin IC   Yufuin Station

Oita Expressway

JR Nippo Main Line

Higashi-Kyushu Expressway

JR Kyudai Line

Oita Prefecture

Iida Highland

Mt. Waita ▲

Tadewara Marsh   •Oike

Chojabaru•

Mt. Kuroiwa ▲   Bogatsuru Marsh

Mt. Mimata ▲

Kuju Mountain range

Kuju Plateau Road Park

Kikuchi Gorge   •Aso-Daikanbo

Aso City

Aso-Jinjya Shrine

57

Aso Station   •Koga Fall

Kumamoto Prefecture

JR Hohi main line

Mt. Kinejima ▲   Mt. Aso   Mt. Taka

Kusasenri-ga-hama

Mt. Eboshi ▲   Mt. Naka   Mt. Neko

•Jigoku Tarutama

Shirakawa Headspring

•Aso-Kumamoto Airport

Minami-Aso Line   •Takamori Station

0   5km

Fukuoka

Oita Airport•

Aso-Kumamoto Airport

Oita   Oita

Kumamoto

Kumamoto   Miyazaki

Rape blossoms and the Isshingyo Ozakura (large cherry blossom tree) in Minamiaso Village. The view evokes a sense of spring.

While preserving this beautiful grass landscape, the people of the area have also developed various products such as Akaushi Beef (Japanese Brown Beef).

In addition to exploring the majestic landscape by walking around billowing volcanoes, hills colored with extensive colonies of Kyushu azaleas (Miyamakirishima) and fall foliage, as well as the grasslands and wetlands that surround them, there are also a great variety of activities to enjoy that are unique to this region, such as taking in the view from paragliders and hot air balloons.

Plentiful spring water— bounties of volcanoes

The plains to the north and south of the caldera have extensive rice paddies and farmland. These have also been sustained by volcanoes—

The Kuju Mountain Range is ideal for trekking. Kyushu azaleas blossom all at once from mid-May to mid-June.

a fact that may come as a surprise. The volcanic strata contains a lot of water, as some of the volcanic product form aquifers or underground layers of water-bearing rocks, while the expansive grassland helps absorb rainwater underground. The water then takes around 50 years to well up to the surface, where it has been used as drinking water as well as for agriculture. Famous spring water spots include the cluster of springs in Minamiaso Village and the spring fountains (*mizuki*) of the *monzenmachi* (shrine town) at Aso Shrine.

These abundant springs are what allowed agriculture to develop in the region and many people to inhabit the land despite the lack of any large rivers nearby. In addition to using the spring water to set up irrigation systems, grass from the pastures and organic matter from cattle and horses have been utilized as compost to make steady improvements to the soil over time, allowing agriculture to flourish.

Nature can at times be a menace. But instead of viewing it solely as a menace, people can learn to get along with it as something to receive bounties from. Aso-Kuju National Park is a place that allows you to get a feel for such a Japanese view of nature.

Shirakawa Headspring (part of the Minamiaso Village spring cluster), where rainwater from the caldera as well as subterranean river water gather.

sciencecolumn

Understanding the Japanese archipelago from a geological standpoint:
What helps create the rich tapestry of diverse landscapes in Japan?

By Yukiyasu Tsutsumi
Department of Geology and Paleontology, National Museum of Nature and Science

With diverse climatic zones from subarctic to temperate and subtropical, regions around the country have developed unique natural environments thanks to the wide array of climates and landscapes. Here, we will explore the background behind those natural environments by looking at their geology, which forms the base (foundation) of their landscapes.

The Sea of Japan was created around 15 to 30 million years ago. After the eastern end of the Eurasian continent broke off, this "fragment" was torn away by the spread of this newly-formed sea. The formation of the Sea of Japan caused the fragment (i.e. Japan) to become an archipelago, which after various crustal changes, now exists as a system of five island arcs including the Chishima Arc, Northeast Japan Arc, Southwest Japan Arc, Izu-Bonin Arc, and Ryukyu Arc. As such, the geology of Japan is complex, and although the broad outline of its formation process is becoming clearer, there is endless debate over the details.

The subduction of tectonic plates causes earthquakes and volcanic activity. Japan owes its abundance of volcanoes to the subduction of two oceanic plates—the Pacific Plate and the Philippine Sea Plate. The wild scenes of fiercely active volcanoes and the majestic landscapes created from past volcanic activity elicit wonder in people both within Japan and around the world. It is safe to say volcanoes are responsible for creating many of the landscapes within national parks. In addition, spinal mountain ranges such as the Japanese Alps were created through the east-west compression of the Japanese archipelago by the Pacific Plate, and landscapes such as coastal cliffs and ria coastlines were created through uplift and subsidence on the coast. As you can see, the landscapes of national parks are closely linked to geological activity.

Since the Japanese archipelago exists in a mid-latitude area of the earth as a long, narrow chain of islands stretching north to south, it has nurtured a diverse climate and natural environment. The climate is by and large warm temperate and humid, providing a good balance of sunshine and rain for animals and plants to grow, and the surrounding ocean is also inhabited by

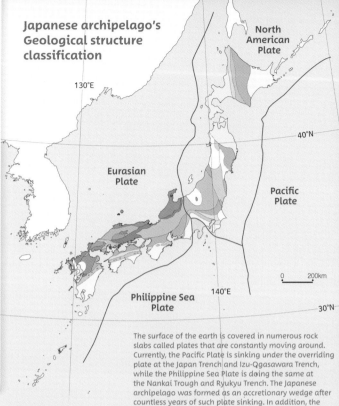

Japanese archipelago's Geological structure classification

130°E
40°N
140°E
30°N

North American Plate

Eurasian Plate

Pacific Plate

Philippine Sea Plate

0   200km

The surface of the earth is covered in numerous rock slabs called plates that are constantly moving around. Currently, the Pacific Plate is sinking under the overriding plate at the Japan Trench and Izu-Ogasawara Trench, while the Philippine Sea Plate is doing the same at the Nankai Trough and Ryukyu Trench. The Japanese archipelago was formed as an accretionary wedge after countless years of such plate sinking. In addition, the compression caused by plate tectonics has contributed to the formation of mountainous regions, ria coastlines, and island-studded landscapes.

diverse marine life. Another one of its appeals is the distinct seasons. In the summer, Japan experiences a unique mugginess due to the warm humid air of the Pacific High. During the winter, the cold dry air of the Siberian High absorbs plenty of water as it crosses the Sea of Japan and causes heavy snowfall on the Sea of Japan coast. A humid wind by itself will not do anything, but the wind hits the mountains and forms clouds, causing rain and snow to fall throughout the region. As you can see, the climate and seasons of Japan are intimately linked to the Pacific Ocean and Sea of Japan, as well as the spinal mountain range that runs down the middle of

the archipelago. Such landscapes as rivers, lakes, and waterfalls formed by the tranquil and sometimes roaring supplies of abundant water—an indispensable part of any national park—also owe their existence to this spinal mountain range created from plate activity. Japan's water, by the way, is mostly soft water. This is due to the precipitous terrain, which only allows rainwater to stay underground for short amounts of time, and the general dearth of lime matter in its geology.

Even within the same region, the landscape changes from season to season, which in turn, changes the kind of food you can enjoy. There are also plenty of areas that flow with hot springs. If possible, I would recommend visiting the same area at different times of the year to enjoy an extended stay as you take in these differences.

The ria coastlines of Ago Bay.
(Ise-Shima National Park)
©FUSAO ONO / SEBUN PHOTO / amanaimages

69

Kirishima-
National P

Standing at the center of the park,
Sakurajima allows you to feel the
powerful energy of the earth and
the complexity of nature.

Kinkowan ark

Land where volcanoes and humans coexist

Witness Sakurajima as smoke billows out of it and the city that spreads at its feet. There are over 20 other volcanoes as well where you can encounter crater lakes, fumarolic activity, hot springs, plateaus, ocean calderas, and other majestic scenery that some call a "cross-sectional garden of volcanic terrain." With plenty of seafood and agricultural products as well as a thriving alcohol industry, a visit to this region is sure to drastically change how to view nature.

Kirishima-Kinkowan National Park
29

Hot springs and majestic views of oceans and mountains

Established in 1934, Kirishima-Kinkowan National Park is one of the oldest national parks in the country. The park is broadly divided into the northern and southern areas known as the Kirishima area and Kinkowan area, respectively, which each feature unique landscapes.

The northern Kirishima area has a series of over 20 volcanoes of various sizes where you can see crater lakes, fumarolic activity, hot springs, and plateaus created from volcanic activity, as well as plenty of natural vegetation. The area, which is also referred to as a "cross-sectional garden of volcanic terrain," receives many tourists each year who visit Ebino Highland, Kirishima Onsen hot springs resort, the Takachihogawara plains,

and Kirishima-jingu Shrine. In addition, Mt. Takachihonomine is a mystical mountain that is said to be the site of the legend of Tenson Korin (heavenly descent of Amaterasu's grandson).

The southern Kinkowan area features the still smoking regional symbol of Sakurajima as its center piece, as well as Mt. Kaimondake (924 m above sea level)—also known as Satsuma-Fuji (the Mt. Fuji of Satsuma)—and Lake Ikeda on the Satsuma Peninsula side, and Cape Sata-misaki on the Osumi Peninsula side, where many subtropical plants grow. These, along with the sea inside the bay form a distinctive landscape.

The globally unseen proximity of people's lives to a volcano

Towering over the Kinkowan Bay as it billows smoke, Sakurajima is located just a stone's

Lake Ikeda is the largest caldera lake in the Kyushu region. On the shore of the lake, you can see extensive terraced rice fields.

throw away at 4 km from the downtown area of the prefectural capital (Kagoshima City) populated by around 600,000 people. Close to 5,000 people live around the volcano and lead their day-to-day lives while keeping an eye out for ashfall reports, an environment nearly unseen anywhere else in the world. Residents make a living through agriculture, fishing, and tourism as they sometimes become covered in ash.

Although ashfall is the enemy of agricultural products, the region has also given birth to specialty foods such as Sakurajima radish and Sakurajima komikan oranges, which thrive on volcanic ash soil.

The water filtered in the mountains helps support Minamikyushu's *shochu* culture and also produces high-quality tea leaves.

The most notable bounties of volcanoes are the hot springs that flow out around the region.

Famous hot springs include the Kirishima Onsen hot springs resort, which flows with hot springs of a variety of properties, and Ibusuki Onsen hot springs, which take advantage of the terrain to offer Sunamushiburo (steam sand bath) experiences. Kirishima Onsen hot springs resort is also where the hot spring culture of *Kazokuburo* (family bath) was born, where small groups can enjoy hot springs in a private room. There is also a settlement (Unagi area, Ibusuki City) where each of the households have natural steam ovens called *sume*, which utilize the hot steam rising from the ground.

The proximity of people's lives to volcanoes is one of the major factors that helped give birth to the food cultures and hot spring cultures unique to this park.

Early fall at Mt. Koshiki, one of the mountains surrounding Ebino Highland. At the summit that sits at 1,301 m above sea level, there are grasslands of *susuki* (Japanese silver grass) and a small marsh.

Branding Park

Kirishima-
Kinkowan
National
Park

Fragrant witch hazel sprout in the spring.

73

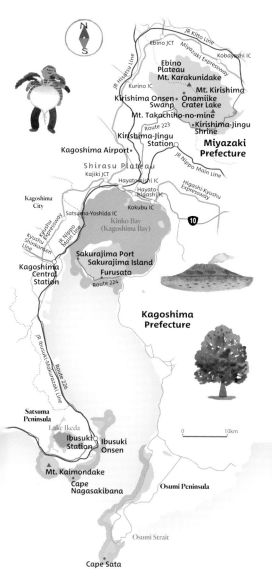

JR Kitto Line
Ebino JCT
Miyazaki Expressway
Kobayashi IC
JR Hisatsu Line

Ebino
Plateau
Mt. Karakunidake

Kurino IC
Mt. Kirishima
Kirishima Onsen • Onamiike
Swamp Crater Lake
Mt. Takachiho-no-mine
• Kirishima-Jingu
Route 223 Shrine
Kirishima-Jingu
Station
Miyazaki
Kagoshima Airport• **Prefecture**

Shirasu Plateau
Kajiki JCT
JR Nippo Main Line
Hayato-nishi IC
Hayato-
higashi IC
Higashi-Kyushu
Expressway

Kagoshima
City
Satsuma-Yoshida IC
Kokubu IC
Kinko Bay
(Kagoshima Bay)
10

Kyushu
Shinkansen
Line
Kyushu
Expressway
JR Nippo
Main Line

Sakurajima Port
Sakurajima Island
Furusato
Route 224

Kagoshima
Central
Station

**Kagoshima
Prefecture**

JR Ibusuki-Makurazaki Line
Route 226

Satsuma
Peninsula
Lake Ikeda
Ibusuki
Station Ibusuki
Onsen

0   10km

Mt. Kaimondake
Cape
Nagasakibana Osumi Peninsula

Osumi Strait

Cape Sata

Kumamoto
Miyazaki

Kagoshima
Miyazaki•
Kagoshima
Airport•
Miyazaki
Bougainvillea
Airport
Kagoshima•

Kinkowan Bay—
an ocean caldera formed
by an eruption

Within the park, you can see volcanoes that continue to erupt to this day—most notably Sakurajima—as well as a group of giant calderas that were formed by past large-scale eruptions. These were created by volcanic activity caused by a plate sinking into the seabed to the east of the Kyushu region, and include the Kakuto, Kobayashi, Aira, and Ata calderas, which stand in a north-to-south line that stretches over the Minamikyushu area.

The Aira caldera, which now forms a deep bay, was created by the collapse of a massive volcano following an eruption and displays one of the most prominent ocean caldera landscapes in the country.

The prefectural capital of Kagoshima City and Sakurajima are only 4 km away.

By the way, as its name suggests, Sakurajima (Sakura Island) used to be an island, until lava flows from a large-scale eruption in 1914 connected it to the Osumi Peninsula.

From experiencing the beautiful volcanic landscapes of Kirishima as well as its legends and culture, to taking in the spectacular views of Sakurajima and Kinkowan Bay as well as the tropical landscapes of the southernmost point of mainland Japan, this place allows you to enjoy a trip full of variety.

The Senjojiki riverbed at Kirishima Onsen hot springs resort. The riverbed is made from lava that cooled and hardened.

Kyushu azalea sprout in early summer. Many can be seen growing around volcanoes.

Ebino Highland is inhabited by wild deer.

Kirishima-Kinkowan National Park

Blessed with a humid climate, Jomonsugi (giant cedar trees) grow tall. Pictured is Wilson's Stump. The tree is estimated to have been 3,000 years old when it was felled.

sciencecolumn

Yakushima— a treasure trove of epiphytes

By Chie Tsutsumi
Department of Botany,
National Museum of Nature and Science

Known for its over 1,000-year-old Jomonsugi (giant cedar trees), the diverse flora of Yakushima Island has led to its designation as a World Natural Heritage. The uniquely humid climate of the island, with an annual rainfall of 1,000 mm at high elevations, has created an environment full of epiphytes.

Containing many mountains over 1000 m including the 1,936-m Mt. Miyanoura within an approximately 132-km perimeter island, Yakushima is inhabited by around 1,500 kinds of tracheophytes and has a condensed population of diverse flora, from subtropical plants to warm and cool-temperate plants, as well as coastal, mountain, river, and marsh plants. Due to its location on the border between subtropical and temperate climatic zones, the island also contains many plants that

Vaccinium yakushimense are designated as an endangered species.

Yakushima goldenrod (*Solidago minutissima*), which is endemic to Yakushima.
©izawa masana / nature pro. / amanaimages

are at the southernmost or northernmost point of their distribution. Some notable aspects of Yakushima are its mountain ranges and rivers that flow through precipitous valleys, landscapes that are rare in southern Japan. In the mountains, you can see dwarfed plants such as Yakushima goldenrod (*Solidago minutissima*) and dwarf creeping jenny (*Lysimachia japonica* var. *minutissima*), while the precipitous rivers offer rheophytes such as Satsuki azaleas and *Hydrobryum puncticulatum*, a kind of riverweed. The number of endemic species that can only be seen in Yakushima is over 70, and many plants are named after the island. A study of endemic plant distribution in Japan conducted by the National Museum of Nature and Science found that Yakushima is second after the Chichi-jima Islands (Ogasawara Islands) in terms of its endemic species index. This illustrates just how plant-rich and valuable the island of Yakushima is.

Yakushima is also a treasure trove of epiphytes. Epiphytes are plants that grow on the surface of other trees. In Yakushima, you can see orchids such as Sekkoku and squirrel's foot fern grow on trees all around the island, along with plants that normally grow on the ground in other regions, such as Japanese cedar, *Trochodendron*, Japanese rowan, and *Rhododendron tashiroi Maxim*. Yakushima experiences such heavy rainfall that it is said to experience "35 days of rain a month." This abundant rain, as well as the misty, humid environment, likely contribute to plants becoming epiphytic. When you visit Yakushima, I would definitely recommend keeping an eye out for tree surfaces.

Vaccinium yakushimense, which I have provided a picture of, belong to the *Vaccinium* genus of the heath family and are epiphytic plants endemic to Yakushima that mostly grow on large moss-laden trees such as Japanese cedars. Although they are categorized as a vulnerable species, you will likely be able to find some even along hiking trails if you pay attention to the tree surfaces at relatively high elevations. The plant is a small, bright green shrub with young branches that are also green, and from around April to May, cute little reddish bell-shaped flowers around 5 to 6 mm in size sprout from between the leaves

In Yakushima, even Japanese rowans are epiphytic.
©higeta norizo / nature pro. / amanaimages

as if hiding among them. In the fall, they grow blackish purple berries. Research has found that *Vaccinium yakushimense* are close relatives of the warm to cool-temperate *Vaccinium smallii* and *Vaccinium hirtum* plants which grow on the ground, and are believed to have evolved to grow on trees thanks to the unique environment of Yakushima.

According to a study of endangered species distribution conducted at the Museum, Yakushima, at over 60 endangered species, has the third most endangered species in Japan after the Chichi-jima Islands in the Ogasawara Islands and Ishigaki-jima Island. One of the reasons why Yakushima has so many endangered species is the damage caused by deer feeding on them. In a 2019 study of endangered ferns, species such as *Thelypteris gracilescens* and *Athyrium yakusimense*, plants commonly seen growing on the ground in the past, are now only seen within areas surrounded by protective fences to keep out deer, but hardly anywhere else. Protecting Yakushima's abundant plant life is the most important issue facing us right now.

Keramashoto

The view from Takatsukiyama
Observatory on Zamami-jima Island.
Footpaths are set up around the
observatory.

**Keramashoto
National Park**
33

National Park

Branding Park

Oceans of Kerama Blue and island time

Although
the Keramashoto Islands,
which consist of Zamami-jima,
Aka-jima, Tokashiki-jima,
and Geruma-jima Islands
among others,
can be visited on a day trip
from Naha on
the main island of Okinawa,
this place deserves
an extended stay.
Let the cobalt blue sea
and leisurely island time
reverberate
to the depths of your soul.

Green sea turtles are the most frequently
encountered type of sea turtle.

Oceans of "Kerama Blue" that nurture life

The Keramashoto Islands consist of around 30 islands of various sizes and numerous reefs. The islands are easily accessible, at just an approximately 35 to 50-minute high-speed ferry ride from Tomari Port in Naha City. Its sparkling oceans known as "Kerama Blue" gradate from a clear light blue to a deep ultramarine.

The Kerama Blue oceans are a cradle of life. The waters surrounding the islands are densely populated with coral of various shapes including table coral, branch coral, horned coral, and rock coral for a total of 248 variations. Around 60 percent of all reef-building coral observable in Japan inhabit these waters.

The complex, three-dimensional structures of such coral attract a lot of marine life. Sea turtles leisurely swim among colorful fish, and from winter to spring, the surrounding waters are visited by humpback whales which come here to breed.

There is more to enjoy than water activities in Kerama. If you turn toward the interior of the island, you can enjoy diverse landscapes that run from the ocean to dry land, which are alive with a folk culture that has been nurtured by a long history. This park allows you to surrender yourself to the relaxed pace of island time and get in touch with your true self in an environment away from everyday life.

Kuro Island

Zamami Island
Ama Beach
Takatsukiyama Observatory
Kozamami Beach
Yakabi Island
Nishibama Beach
Aka Island
Geruma Island
Kora-ke
Kuba Island
Kerama Airport
Fukaji Island

Gishippu Island

Okiyama Rock

Tokashiki Port
Tokashiki Island
Tokashiku Beach

Aharen Beach

Cape Aharen Garden

Maejima Island

Hatejima Island
Nakajima Island
Ugamijima Island

Kamiyama Island
Nagannu Island
Keise Island(Chibishi)
Kuefu Island

0 ————— 5km

East China Sea

Okinawa

Nahatomari Port
Naha Airport

Pacific Ocean

Nishibama Terrace at Nishibama Beach on Aka-jima Island.

An "island time" that invites you to a retreat

"Retreat" originally means "to run" or "to seek refuge." As a derivation from this, it is also used to denote a time away from the bustle of daily life where you can reset your mind and body, and restart your daily life with a positive outlook. The islands of Kerama are full of beautiful, dramatic landscapes and soothing experiences that invite visitors to go on a retreat.

The Tokashiki-jima, Zamami-jima, Aka-jima, and Geruma-jima Islands each have appealing observatories which give you a full view of the dynamic island-studded landscape. The sunset views from such high grounds are

The Takara Residence on Geruma-jima Island retains the prototypical style of a traditional Okinawan house and is designated as a National Important Cultural Property.

As you watch the sun set slowly into the ocean from beaches and observatories, you will be momentarily transported to another world.

You can look forward to whale watching during the winter. With enough luck, you may encounter a mother whale and her calf.

In Okinawa, there is a custom called yuntaku where friends and family gather under the shade of trees to enjoy a chat as they cool off in the evening breeze. Passing through the alleys of villages lined with limestone walls and coral fences in the evening and enjoying a relaxed moment of island time as you join in people's yuntaku circles is another experience you can only get on these remote islands. Before you know it, star-studded skies will have spread up above.

Sea kayaking and whale watching

A registered wetland under the Ramsar Convention, the oceans here have some of the highest transparency in the world and a great variety of marine life including fish and coral.

One creature that is often encountered while scuba diving or snorkeling is a variety of sea turtles. The oceans of Kerama are inhabited by green sea turtles and hawksbill sea turtles, which you can see swimming through the

so beautiful that they will make you forget the time. Lounging on the sand at Aharen Beach (Tokashiki-jima Island) and Ama Beach (Zamami-jima Island) as you look out at the ocean and spend an evening watching the sunset as the ocean and sky change color with each passing moment is enough to refresh both the mind and body.

The Umi-Ugan Festival (Kaijin-sai) on Zamami-jima Island where people pray for safety at sea and a bountiful harvest. Okinawan god Miruku (Bodhisattva Miroku) leads the procession.

The highly transparent seas are a world-class diving spot where colorful tropical fish dance around coral reefs.

ocean from sea kayaks and by SUP (stand up paddleboarding).

From late December to early April each year, there is also a good chance you can see humpback whales, which visit Kerama's oceans during that time to breed. Whale watching tours where you can observe these mystical humpback whales in nature from a boat are a popular winter activity. If you are lucky enough, you may be able to observe the child-rearing scenes of these whales.

Notably, the people who run these water activities make the preservation of wildlife the forefront of their concern as they go about their work. The businesses collaborate with local residents to help protect the ocean environment, engaging in preservation efforts and monitoring surveys of the coral, and volunteering to clean up the beaches.

The oceans of Kerama Blue, a treasure trove of diverse creatures, are thus protected through community-wide preservation efforts.

©Jiro Tateno / SEBUN PHOTO / amanaimages

The rare animals that color the Amami Islands

By Masanori Nakae

Department of Zoology,
National Museum of Nature and Science

Take a trip to go see rare animals in Amami-Oshima Island and other places in the Amami Islands, which are known as a "Galapagos of the East" for their many endemic plants and animals.

The Amami Islands are located in southern Kagoshima Prefecture and consist of islands such as the Amami-Oshima, Kakeromajima, Ukejima, Yorojima, Kikaijima, Tokunoshima, Okinoerabujima, and Yoronjima Islands. Various endemic and rare animals live amid the rich nature of the islands, including its subtropical laurel forests, mangrove forests, mudflats, and coral reefs. Here, I will introduce our readers to a few of the animals that any visitor to Amamigunto National Park will want to see.

The Amami rabbit is an endemic species that you will not find anywhere else in the world outside of the Amami-Oshima and Tokunoshima Islands. Although they are more or less the same size as Japanese hares, they have characteristic blackish-brown fur and shorter ears and legs. Since they are nocturnal, there is a chance you might encounter them in forests of evergreen, broad-leaved trees at night. Partly due to their display of primitive rabbit characteristics, the species is considered scientifically important, and their low population among other reasons have led to their designation as National Special Natural Monuments in 1963 as well as "nationally endangered species of wild fauna and flora" under the Law for the Conservation of Endangered Species of Wild Fauna and Flora in 2004, and today are categorized as endangered under the Red List of the Ministry of the Environment (but thanks to preservation efforts, they have started to regain their population).

The Amami jay is another endemic species that cannot be found anywhere in the world outside of the Amami-Oshima, Kakeromajima,

The extensive mangrove forests in the village of Sumiyo on Amami-Oshima Island.

The Amami rabbit is covered in blackish-brown fur.
©TAKESHI FUKAZAWA / SEBUN PHOTO / amanaimages

The Amami jay is designated as the official prefectural bird of Kagoshima Prefecture.
©TOSHITAKA MORITA / SEBUN PHOTO / amanaimages

and Ukejima Islands. This beautiful bird has a reddish-brown body and a bright blue head, wings, and tail, and was designated as a National Natural Monument in 1921. The species was previously on the brink of extinction due to the destruction of their habitat by land development and being preyed on by mongooses and feral cats, but thanks to preservation efforts, have started to regain their population and were even removed from the list of nationally endangered species of wild fauna and flora in 2008. Their main habitat is natural laurel forest, but there is a chance you can also encounter them at the edge of these forests.

There are also creatures on the Amami Islands that you both would and would not want to encounter. Those include poisonous *habu* and *hime habu* vipers. Habu are a species endemic to the Central Ryukyu islands of Amami-Oshima, Tokunoshima, and Okinawa Islands and at over 2 m long, are the largest poisonous snakes in Japan. In recent years, there have been around 50 annual reports of biting incidents in the Amami Islands. Sometimes, you will see sticks around 2 m in length sitting by the road on the Amami-Oshima and Kakeromajima Islands. These are meant to be used for protection against habu.

In addition to the creatures mentioned above, there are also; Amami woodcock, which have charming, rather squat bodies; the Amami thrush, which is a subspecies of scaly thrush and a large bird (around 30 cm) within the thrush family; Amami Ishikawa's frog, which are considered the most beautiful frog in Japan; Otton frog, which grow to over 10 cm in length; white-spotted pufferfish, which are known to form crop circle-like, circular patterns at the bottom of the sea and Ryukyu-*ayu* fish, whose only natural habitat in the world is Amami-Oshima Island (the population seen on Okinawa Island was brought over from Amami-Oshima). There are so many endemic species that inhabit the Amami Islands and their surrounding areas that it is impossible to introduce them all in this article. I would recommend paying a visit to the islands where these animals live to get a first-hand feel of why they are inhabited by so many endemic species and whether the future is bright for them.

Environmental issues—a threat to the earth and to national parks

Afterword

By Masato Morikawa
Visitor Use Promotion Office,
National Park Division,
Nature Conservation Bureau,
Ministry of the Environment

As has been discussed so far, Japan's national parks feature unique landscapes created by the nature and culture of each region. However, the effects of global environmental issues such as global warming, ocean plastic pollution, and decreased biodiversity due to species extinction, are beginning to appear in national parks as well.

In October 2018, the Intergovernmental Panel on Climate Change (IPCC) released a special report entitled "Global Warming of 1.5°C," which made further warnings to countries around the world. In Japan's national parks, multiple regions in recent years have reported increasing cases of damage to alpine plants from being eaten by *shika* deer. It has been pointed out that shika deer habitats are affected by the amount of snowfall, and it is possible that decreased snowfall due to global warming may be contributing to the expansion of the deer's habitat into alpine belts. Alpine plants are an important component of the spring and summer landscapes of these areas. Also, a decrease in snowfall may force regions where winter sports have been enjoyed over the years to reevaluate the way those activities are enjoyed.

In addition, national parks with coastlines are plagued by ocean plastic pollution. The beautiful ocean landscapes of Iriomote-Ishigaki National Park are affected by the marine debris that periodically washes up on its beaches. In the future, the oceans that surround Japan and the rich marine ecosystem contained within them are feared to be affected by microplastics.

In terms of biodiversity, an estimated one million species around the world are in danger of extinction according to the Global

Assessment Report released in May 2019 by the Intergovernmental Science-Policy Platform on Biodiversity and Ecosystem Services (IPBES), which warns that many of these species could go extinct within a few decades if we do not remove threats from human activity. In Japan's national parks, too, the biodiversity of various regions is being affected by man-made causes. For example, in Ogasawara National Park, which features a unique biodiversity fostered by the islands' long isolated environment, endemic species that inhabit the Ogasawara Islands, especially insects such as Ogasawara shijimi butterflies and Ogasawara dragonflies, are in danger of going extinct from being preyed upon by green anoles, an invasive lizard species introduced to the islands by humans.

The threats to national parks mentioned above are all serious issues that are being addressed in each region by the Ministry of the Environment in collaboration with interested parties. When visiting Japan's national parks, I encourage you to turn your eyes to the threats they are facing as well as the nature, culture, and other appealing aspects of the park.

Due to its unique geographical environment, Japan faces constant threats from natural disasters such as earthquakes, volcanic eruptions, and typhoons. But this environment is also what helped form its unique landscapes unseen anywhere else in the world and allowed the people who live there to carry on the wisdom of their ancestors, maintain a strong connection to the nature in their region, and develop a unique culture. Many national parks in Japan are located in such regions.

Over the years, the population has increasingly concentrated in cities, and the people who live in cities have lost touch with nature, a tendency which continues to grow. In such an age, my hope is that more people will experience national parks not simply as tourist destinations, but also as a place with magnificent natural environments containing ecosystems that are both flexible and whose functions help support human life, as well as a source of inspiration for how to live alongside nature.

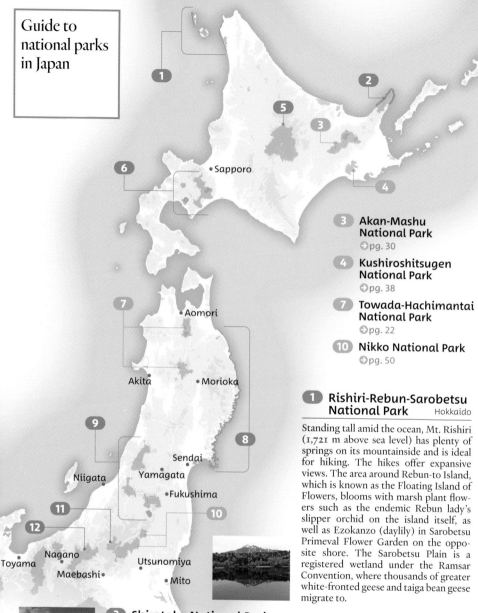

Guide to national parks in Japan

• Sapporo

3 Akan-Mashu
National Park
⊃pg. 30

4 Kushiroshitsugen
National Park
⊃pg. 38

7 Towada-Hachimantai
National Park
⊃pg. 22

10 Nikko National Park
⊃pg. 50

• Aomori

Akita • Morioka

Sendai
Yamagata
• Fukushima

Niigata

Toyama
Nagano
Maebashi•
Utsunomiya
• Mito

1 Rishiri-Rebun-Sarobetsu National Park   *Hokkaido*

Standing tall amid the ocean, Mt. Rishiri (1,721 m above sea level) has plenty of springs on its mountainside and is ideal for hiking. The hikes offer expansive views. The area around Rebun-to Island, which is known as the Floating Island of Flowers, blooms with marsh plant flowers such as the endemic Rebun lady's slipper orchid on the island itself, as well as Ezokanzo (daylily) in Sarobetsu Primeval Flower Garden on the opposite shore. The Sarobetsu Plain is a registered wetland under the Ramsar Convention, where thousands of greater white-fronted geese and taiga bean geese migrate to.

2 Shiretoko National Park   *Hokkaido*

Attractive aspects of this park include its majestic landscapes of mountain ranges formed by volcanoes and coastal cliffs over 100 m tall. In the park, you can see alpine plants including rare species such as *Viola kitamiana* (a kind of violet) as well as brown bears. Whale watching tours in Rausu allow you to see different kinds of whales depending on the season, starting with common minke whales in the spring, then killer whales and sperm whales later in the year. During the winter there are also drift ice cruises. The park is registered as a World Natural Heritage for its biodiversity and ecosystem.

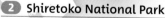

⑤ Daisetsuzan National Park Hokkaido

Daisetsuzan is the largest mountainous national park in Japan where the Daisetsuzan and Tokachi volcanic groups sit on top of a lava plateau along with an extensive mixed coniferous forest. Permafrost and snowy gorges can be seen within the alpine belt where mountains of around 2,000 m form a mountain range. The park allows you to enjoy the full spectrum of nature with its treasure trove of as many as 250 kinds of alpine plants; rare animal species such as Japanese pikas—which can only be seen in rocky areas—and the high-altitude butterfly Eversmann's parnassian; as well as hiking, hot springs, and skiing.

⑥ Shikotsu-Toya National Park Hokkaido

A "Museum of Volcanic Activity" where you can see distinctive volcanic landscapes such as the two large caldera lakes of Lake Shikotsu and Lake Toya, volcanoes of various forms such as Mt. Yotei, Mt. Usuzan, and Mt. Tarumae, as well as fountains, Jigokudani (Hell Valley), and volcanic lakes. Lake Shikotsu, whose water is notably deep and calm, is the northernmost lake in Japan that does not freeze over. At Mt. Yotei, you can see a textbook case of vertical plant distribution with a forest that ranges from broad-leaved trees to coniferous trees to alpine plants. The Lake Toya and Mt. Usuzan area has been recognized as the Toya-Usu UNESCO Global Geopark.

⑧ Sanriku Fukko (reconstruction) National Park Aomori, Iwate, and Miyagi

This park extends 250 km north to south from the Tanesashi Coast in Aomori to Mt. Kinkasan in Miyagi. The southern part of the park features ria coastlines formed by coastal erosion. There are also plenty of fishing ports where you can enjoy distinctive landscapes where grand, yet elegant coastlines exist alongside signs of human activity that have coexisted with nature. On the coast, there are breeding grounds for seabirds such as streaked shearwaters and flowers such as beach roses and *Lilium maculatum* (see-through lily). Part of the purpose of this national park is to help the area recover from the 2011 Tohoku earthquake.

⑨ Bandai-Asahi National Park Yamagata, Fukushima, and Niigata

In the three sacred mountains of Dewasanzan, you can encounter old shrines and mountain ascetics. The park also features the Tohoku Alps, an area stretching from the Asahi Mountain Range to the Iide Mountain Range which blooms with *Lilium maculatum* and *Gentiana nipponica* var. *robusta* (a kind of gentian flower); the Azuma Mountain Range, where you can enjoy hiking, skiing, and hot springs; Mt. Bandai, which is surrounded by over 300 lakes including Goshiki Pond and Lake Hibara; and Lake Inawashiro, a stopover site for tundra swans. Each region has its own unique appeal in this expansive mountain park.

⑪ Oze National Park Fukushima, Tochigi, Gunma, and Niigata

This park consists of the Ozegahara Plateau (1878 acres), a high moor sitting at an altitude of 1,400 m; Lake Ozenuma, a volcanic dammed lake; and mountains over 2,000 m such as Mt. Shibutsu, Mt. Hiuchigatake, Mt. Aizu-Komagatake, and Mt. Tashiro. The park is inhabited by 938 kinds of plants including northern plants and rare species such as *Japonolirion*. Wooden footpaths are set up in the wetlands where you can go for a hike as you enjoy views of white skunk cabbages and broad dwarf day lilies. The wetlands are registered under the Ramsar Convention.

⑫ Joshin'etsukogen National Park Gunma, Niigata, and Nagano

This park contains many mountains included in the "100 finest mountains of Japan" such as Mt. Asama and Mt. Tanigawa. The area also encompasses ski resorts such as Naeba and Shiga Kogen, as well as many of the most famous hot spring spots in Japan such as Shima Onsen, Kusatsu Onsen, and Manza Onsen. In addition to a great number of alpine plants including *komakusa*, the park is also inhabited by birds of prey such as golden eagles and mountain hawk-eagles, as well as Asiatic black bears, Japanese serow, and stoats. The snow monkeys of Jigokudani Yaen-Koen are a must-see.

20 Ise-Shima National Park
↪ pg. 56

Toyama
Kanazawa
Nagano
Utsunomiya
Maebashi
Mito
22
Fukui
19
14
Saitama
18
17
Tokyo
Chiba
Matsue Tottori
Kofu
Yokohama
Gifu
Nagoya
Kyoto Otsu
Shizuoka
Kobe
Nara Tsu
Hiroshima
Okayama
Osaka
16
Takamatsu
Wakayama
Tokushima
20
Matsuyama
Kochi
21

13 Myoko-Togakushi renzan National Park
Niigata and Nagano

A unique mountainous area where the active volcanoes of Mt. Myoko and Mt. Yakeyama stand near the non-volcanic Togakushi Mountain Range. At Itoigawa Geopark, you can observe the western fault lines of the Fossa Magna. Lake Nojiri, which was formed by landslides at Mt. Kurohime, has intricate lakeshores. Togakushi Highland is a famous birdwatching site where you can observe over 100 kinds of wild birds including the narcissus flycatcher, white-backed woodpecker, and ruddy kingfisher.

14 Chichibu-Tama-Kai National Park
Saitama, Tokyo, Yamanashi, and Nagano

The closest mountain park to Tokyo. Some characteristics of the park include the Okuchichibu Mountains, where high peaks over 2,000 m stretch from the mountain range in Okutama; the mountainous area encompassing Daibosatsu Pass and Mt. Ryokami; and variegated gorges. The area forms the headwaters of rivers such as Tama River and Arakawa River and features beautiful gorges as well as abundant flora. The dense forest environment has nurtured many large animals and the rivers are a treasure trove of char and cherry salmon. You can also enjoy hikes along the peaks of the mountains.

15

15 Ogasawara National Park   Tokyo

A group of subtropical oceanic islands that lie approximately 1,000 km south of the Japanese mainland. The park has been designated a World Natural Heritage for the unique way its plants and animals have evolved and its treasure trove of endemic species. The islands are inhabited by rare endangered species such as the Japanese wood pigeon and the Ogasawara giant bat. The surrounding waters of the islands are inhabited by coral and tropical fish. You can also encounter humpback whales, Indo-Pacific bottlenose dolphins, and green sea turtles.

16 Fuji-Hakone-Izu National Park
Tokyo, Kanagawa, Yamanashi, and Shizuoka

Mt. Fuji, the highest peak in Japan (3,776 m), is surrounded by the Fuji Goko Lakes and dense forests as well as lakes of spring water and waterfalls. To access the steaming Owakudani Valley in Hakone as well as the numerous hot springs in the area, you can take the Hakone Tozan Railway (mountain railway) or the ropeway. In the Izu Peninsula, which has forests and diverse coastlines, you can enjoy hiking, water sports, and fresh seafood. The Izu Islands have plenty of spots for fishing and scuba diving. This is a highly accessible national park close to the Tokyo Metropolis.

17 Chubusangaku National Park
Niigata, Toyama, Nagano, and Gifu

One of the most outstanding and famous mountain landscapes in Japan with numerous mountains over 3,000 m such as Mt. Shirouma, Mt. Tateyama, Mt. Yarigatake, and Mt. Norikura. Hikers will marvel at the deep U-shaped valleys shaved away by glaciers and the beautiful snowy gorges. The park is inhabited by many mammals such as Asiatic black bears, Japanese serow, and stoats, birds of prey, and high-altitude butterflies. In the alpine belt, you can encounter creeping pines (*Pinus pumila*) and rare rock ptarmigans (a type of grouse) within its flower fields.

18 Hakusan National Park
Toyama, Ishikawa, Fukui, and Gifu

With Gozengamine (2,702 m) as its highest peak, the Hakusan Mountain Range is known for its sacred mountains. Primeval nature remains within the alpine and sub-alpine belts of the park, which are inhabited by as many as 250 kinds of alpine plants including Hakusan *furo* (*Geranium nipponicum*) and chocolate lilies. The park also has abundant fauna and is designated as a Biosphere Reserve by UNESCO. High altitude areas feature natural landscapes formed by what is said to be 600 million tons of heavy snowfall. In addition, many dinosaur fossils are found at the Tetori Group, a series of formations around Hakusan.

19 Minami Alps National Park
Yamanashi, Nagano, and Shizuoka

The park consists of non-volcanic mountains which continue to rise to this day including the Kaikoma and Hoo Mountains, Shirane Mountains (whose highest peak is the 3,193-m Mt. Kitadake, the second highest mountain in the country), and the Akaishi Mountains. Within the park, you can see many cirques, V-shaped valleys, and landslide scars formed by glaciers. Due to the climate and the terrain, the tree lines in these mountains are at a high altitude, and the forests extend to the ridgelines. The area features plants that have survived since the ice age such as *Callianthemum hondoense* and eight-petal mountain-avens, as well as high-altitude butterflies such as orange tips.

21 Yoshino-Kumano National Park
Mie, Nara, and Wakayama

The park features the Omine Mountain Range and Odaigahara, a plateau covered in extensive beech forests, as well as the beautiful deep valleys of Kumano River, which flows from such highlands. The coastal areas have many sea cliffs, and these intricate coastal landforms serve as an excellent breeding ground for seabirds. Pacific reef herons and Pacific swifts can be observed along the shoreline from Kumano to Owase. The "Sacred Sites and Pilgrimage Routes in the Kii Mountain Range" are a World Cultural Heritage known since ancient times for the worship of the three deities of Kumano and as holy sites of *shugendo* mountain asceticism. Mt. Yoshino is one of the most famous wild cherry tree viewing spots in Japan.

22 San'inkaigan National Park
Kyoto, Hyogo, and Tottori

This park is known as the "Museum of Coastal Landforms" for its diverse array of landforms including sea cliffs, sea caves, reefs, and sand dunes. The coast is also recognized as the "San'in Kaigan Global Geopark." The intricate landforms of the ria coastlines form a unique contrast with the sand dunes at the river mouth. Sand dune plants such as *Pseudolysimachion ornatum* and Japanese sedge can be seen at Tango Sand Dunes and Tottori Sand Dunes. The oceans have a high transparency and beautiful underwater landscapes such as kelp forests.

23 Setonaikai National Park

Eleven prefectures along the coast of
the Seto Inland Sea

The extensive inland sea stretching from the
Osaka Bay to Kanmon Strait and Kunisaki
Peninsula is dotted with many islands. The
coast offers expansive views of terraced
fields, harbor towns where boats wait for
the tide to come in, shrines and temples,
and other landscapes where people have
led their lives since ancient times. The seas,
which are separated from open water by
straits, have abundant seafood and nurture
rare creatures such as finless porpoises and
Japanese horseshoe crabs. Itsukushima-
jinja Shrine on Miyajima Island is registered
as a World Cultural Heritage along with the
Misen Primeval Forest that grows in the
interior of the island.

24 Daisen-Oki National Park
⊃ pg. 8

28 Aso-Kuju National Park
⊃ pg. 62

29 Kirishima-Kinkowan
National Park
⊃ pg. 70

33 Keramashoto
National Park
⊃ pg. 78

25 Ashizuri-Uwakai National Park

Ehime and Kochi

The Ashizuri area offers views of precipitous cliffs that stretch all along the coast,
while the Uwakai area has ria coastlines with intricate inlets and seas dotted with
islands both big and small. Subtropical marine life and colonies of coral can be
seen in both areas due to the warm Kuroshio Current, including leaf coral colonies that can extend to over 50 m wide. Nametoko Gorge located in the upstream
area of the inland Shimanto river system has beautifully smooth riverbeds.

26 Saikai National Park Nagasaki

An ocean park made up of around 400 islands stretching from the Kujuku Shima Islands in Sasebo and Hirado-jima Island to the Goto Islands. The park features diverse coastal landscapes and ecosystems. It is also a stopover site where you can observe migratory birds such as crested honey buzzards, Chinese sparrowhawks, hooded cranes, and white-naped cranes. The area has historically been exposed to Chinese and European culture, and overlaps with World Cultural Heritage Site "Hidden Christian Sites in the Nagasaki Region." The area's whaling culture and military ruins in Sasebo are also worth exploring.

27 Unzen-Amakusa National Park Nagasaki, Kumamoto, and Kagoshima

Mt. Fugen in Unzen formed Mt. Heisei-shinzan (1,483 m) after experiencing massive eruptions from 1990 to 1995. The Shimabara Peninsula has been recognized as a Global Geopark for its abundant volcanoes, hot springs, and springs. At Mt. Fugen, you can also enjoy forests full of trees that change colors, flowers such as Kyushu azaleas, and summer birds such as blue-and-white flycatchers and Himalayan cuckoos. The Amakusa area features an island-studded ocean with 120 islands of various sizes and a wide variety of landscapes such as embayments characteristic of submerged shorelines, land-tied islands, and sea cliffs, as well as coral in its seas.

30 Yakushima (Island) National Park Kagoshima

Yakushima, a mountainous island that experiences the most rainfall in Japan, encompasses climates from subtropical to warm and cool-temperate, and is home to a diverse array of flora that inhabit altitudes anywhere from 0 to 1,900 m. Towering Yakusugi trees over 1,000 years old grow on the island, which are registered as a World Natural Heritage. If you go trekking, you can enjoy primeval forests and gorges covered in moss, and grasslands that bloom with *Rhododendron yakushimanum* around the summits. The volcanic Kuchinoerabu-jima Island has hot springs of various properties, and is inhabited by the rare Erabu flying fox.

31 Amamigunto National Park Kagoshima

The Amami Islands are a group of islands consisting of the mountainous Amami-Oshima and Tokunoshima Islands, and the flat Kikaijima, Okinoerabujima, and Yoronjima Islands. The islands are covered in subtropical laurel forests and inhabited by endemic plants such as *Lilium alexandrae* (a type of lily) and *Calanthe tokunoshimensis* (a type of orchid), as well as rare animals such as the Amami rabbit. In the Kinsakubaru Native Forest on Amami-Oshima Island, you can see flying spider-monkey tree ferns. Snorkeling among coral reefs on the Tokunoshima and Yoronjima Islands is also enjoyable. You can also enjoy the unique island culture of people living amid the sea.

32 Yambaru National Park Okinawa

"Yambaru" refers to the subtropical laurel forest belt that extends over the northern part of the main Okinawa island. The park offers diverse natural landscapes including sea cliffs of limestone, karst landforms, and mangrove forests. The Yambaru area is blessed with high biodiversity and is inhabited by endemic species such as birds including Okinawa rails, Ishikawa's frogs, and Yanbaru long-armed scarab beetles. The park offers guided trekking and canoe tours.

34 Iriomote-Ishigaki National Park Okinawa

The southernmost national park in Japan. Iriomote-jima Island has the largest mangrove forest in the country where plenty of canoe tours are offered. The subtropical forests are inhabited by rare wild animals such as the Iriomote wild cat and the crested serpent eagle. Ishigaki-jima Island and Iriomote-jima Island are separated by the largest coral reef in Japan where you can also observe majestic reef manta rays.

With the Tokyo 2020 Olympic and Paralympic Games serving as its impetus, the Japan Cultural Expo is a festival of culture and art seeking to—under the overall theme of Humanity and Nature—communicate the Japanese sense of beauty that permeates Japanese culture and art around the country to domestic and international audiences as well as the next generation in the hope that this will open the door to a new future.

For over 10,000 years since the prehistoric Jomon period, the Japanese people have valued a diverse nature and believed that life resides within its every corner. They have expressed a spirit of reverence for such life through their culture and art as well as their way of life.

The various art forms of Japan—from Jomon-period pottery to sculptures such as Buddha statues, paintings such as ukiyo-e and *byobu* folding screens, traditional crafts such as lacquerware, textiles such as kimono, famous traditional performing arts such as *noh* and *kabuki*, literature, manga, and anime—also reflect the natural environment of this country and the way the Japanese view nature. The Japanese people have also embodied a spirit of resonance and empathy with nature through their clothing, food, housing and other aspects of their way of life or lifestyle and have valued such a sense of beauty.

By introducing the long line of culture and art that stretches from the Jomon period to the present, we hope that the festival will foster interactions between people and evoke excitement, leading to a respect for diversity around the world, a sharing of our universal humanity, and an aspiration for world peace.

Agency for Cultural Affairs
Japan Arts Council

information

Ministry of the Environment Government of Japan

(English)

Facebook
https://www.facebook.com/NationalParksOfJapan
Instagram
https://www.instagram.com/nationalpark_japan
JNTO
https://www.japan.travel/national-parks

(Japanease)

Facebook
https://www.facebook.com/KankyoJpn.gov
Ministry of the Environment
Government of Japan website
https://www.env.go.jp/park

Daisen

Daisen National Park Centre
40-33 Daisen, Daisen Town, Saihaku County,
Tottori Prefecture
https://tottoridaisen.web.fc2.com
Ogamiyama-Jinjya-okunomiya
Daisen, Daisen Town, Saihaku County,
Tottori Prefecture
www.oogamiyama.or.jp
Association for Preservation of
the Mt. Daisen summit
40-33 Daisen, Daisen Town, Saihaku County,
Tottori Prefecture
The Hanzaki Research Institute of Japan
https://www.hanzaki.net/
Bushido
https://www.bushidojapan.com/salamander
Tendaishu Bekkakuhonzan
Kakubanzan Daisenjil
58 Daisen, Daisen Town, Saihaku County,
Tottori Prefecture
http://daisenji.jp
Shukubo Kansho-in Sanraku-so
14 Daisen, Daisen Town, Saihaku County,
Tottori Prefecture
https://www.san-raku.jp
IzumoOyashiro shrine
195 Kizukihigashi, Taisha Town, Izumo City,
Tottori Prefecture
http://www.izumooyashiro.or.jp
Izumo-taisha Narrative guide
441-3 kitaaraki, Taisha Town, Izumo City,
Tottori Prefecture
http://www.izumo-kankou.gr.jp
Kokuminshukusha Sanbe-so
2072-1 Shigaku, Sanbe Town, Ohda City,
Shimane Prefecture
https://www.sanbesou.jp

Oki

Sasaki Family Residence
346-2 Imazu, Okinoshima Town, Oki County,
Shimane Prefecture
contact information:
  Okinoshima Town Board of Education
  Social Education Division
  Culture Promotion Section
Cocoro Ryokan
16-2 Higashimachi-Uyanoshimo, Okinoshima Town,
Oki County, Shimane Prefecture
http://cocoro-ryokan.com
Oki Sizenmura
5328-6 Oaza Kaishi, Kaishi Town, Oki County,
Shimane Prefecture
http://www.sizenmura.com
Yawata Kokuyouseki
320 Kumi Okinoshima Town, Oki County,
Shimane Prefecture

Towada

Towadako Guidehouse Kai—(inside Café Ikoi)
486 Yasumiya, Aza Towada-Lakeside, Oaza Okuse,
Towada City, Aomori Prefecture
http://tgkai.jp
Oirase Natural Tourism Resources Study Group
Sangreen103, 11-1 Nishi 23-ban-Cho, Towada City,
Aomori Prefecture
https://www.oiken.org
Craft Shop Yuzuriha
11-253 Aza Tochikubo, Oaza Okuse, Towada City,
Aomori Prefecture
http://www.yuzuriha.jp

Hachimantai

Tamagawa Onsen
Aza Shibukurosawa, Tamagawa, Tazawako,
Senboku City, Akita Prefecture
https://www.tamagawa-onsen.jp
Fukenoyu Onsen
Aza kumazawa Kokuyurin-nai, Hachimantai,
Kazuno City, Akita Prefecture
http://www.fukenoyu.jp

Hokkaido

Kawayu Eco-Museum Center
2-2-6 Kawayu Onsen, Teshikaga Town, Kawakami County,
Hokkaido
https://www.kawayu-eco-museum.com
Akankohan Eco-Museum Center
1-1-1 Akanko Onsen, Akan Town Kushiro City, Hokkaido
http://business4.plala.or.jp/akan-eco
Lake Akan Ainu Theater (Ikoro)
4-7-84 Akanko Onsen, Akan Town, Kushiro City,
Hokkaido
On'nenai Visitor Center
Onnenai, Tsurui Village, Akan County, Hokkaido
http://www.kushiro-shitsugen-np.jp/kansatu/onnenaiv
Lake Toro Eco-Museum Center (Arukotto)
Torogenya Shibecha Town, Kawakami County, Hokkaido
http://www.kushiro-shitsugen-np.jp/kansatu/tooroedo
Tsurui-Ito Tancho Sanctuary
Wild Bird Society of Japan Project Promotion Office
Aza Nakasetsuri Minami, Tsurui Village, Akan County,
Hokkaido
http://park15.wakwak.com/~tancho
Wakkanupuri
6-8 Sawanchisappu, Teshikaga Town, Kawakami County,
Hokkaido
https://wakkanupuri.com

Interviews, Editing, Writing	Nobuko Miyashita (pg. 8-41)
Editing	Nobiru Nakamura (pg. 44-75, 78-83)
	Ippei Aoki (pg. 88-93)
Translation	Arc Communications
Book design, DTP of body text	Kenji Asazuma
Map creation	Atelier Plan
Illustrations	Maki Kobayashi
Proofreading	Akira Yoshino
	Yuriko Matsui
Photography	Susumu Yasui
	Shinsuke Matsukawa
	Natsuko Okada
	Ayako Kubota

Trip to the National Parks of Japan

Copyright© 2020 by Japan International Broadcasting Inc.
ISBN978-4-14-081818-3   C0026
All right reserved.
Published by NHK Publishing, Inc.(NHK Shuppan)
In cooperation with Ministry of the Environment Government of Japan

For information:
NHK Publishing, Inc. (NHK Shuppan)
41-1 Udagawa-cho, Shibuya, Tokyo 150-8081, Japan
http://www.nhk-book.co.jp

Trip to
the National Parks
of
Japan

発行日　2020年5月15日　第1刷発行

企画　日本国際放送
©2020 Japan International Broadcasting Inc.

編集　NHK出版

協力　環境省

発行者　森永公紀

発行所　NHK出版
　〒150-8081　東京都渋谷区宇田川町41-1
　電話　0570-002-143（編集）
　　　　0570-000-321（注文）
　ホームページ　http://www.nhk-book.co.jp
　振替　00110-1-49701

印刷・製本　凸版印刷

Printed in Japan
ISBN978-4-14-081818-3
C0026